Mining Dept.

Bill Aubrey's

Office

BEYOND THE DICTIONARY
IN SPANISH

CASSELL'S

BEYOND THE DICTIONARY IN SPANISH

by

A. BRYSON GERRARD

AND

JOSÉ DE HERAS HERAS

MINERVA PRESS

FUNK & WAGNALLS
A Division of Reader's Digest Books, Inc.

© *Cassell & Co. Ltd., 1953*
First published in the United States in 1964
First paperbound edition published in 1967

Library of Congress Catalogue Card Number: 64-15859

PREFACE

It would be impertinent to produce yet another book on Spanish if it did not offer something not previously obtainable. What this book offers is indicated by its title, viz. particularities of meaning and usage in colloquial speech which no ordinary dictionary could be expected to include but which are essential to the proper speaking of any language. The gap between the written word, as acquired from grammar-books, and the living speech as spoken by a native, is not necessarily a wide one but an inordinate amount of time is often spent in crossing it and perhaps even more in not realising that it is there to be crossed. It is all too easy for a person who has reached a point in his studies where he can understand and make himself understood with ease to imagine that he is doing splendidly, but most of us have met the fluent foreign student who says: 'I am in England since five months; actually I go to the University where I assist at conferences', and we understand him so readily—or we think we do—that it would hardly occur to us to point out that there are five mistakes in that one sentence.

It is quite likely, of course, that the foreign student, if he were writing instead of speaking, would make no mistakes at all and certainly, when speaking a language, one of the difficulties is to remember to use the right word in time. One of the objects of this book is to make you conscious, in time, of the moments when idiomatic words or phrases should be used, to be unconsciously aware of the occasions when the proper translation of 'but', for example, will be *sino*; 'to use', *aprovechar*; 'to realise', *darse cuenta*, etc.

I use the word 'idiomatic' chiefly in the sense that every language is idiomatic. This is not a word-and-phrase book giving you all manner of fancy proverbs and sayings any of which may be used two or three times in your life; it concentrates its attention on words you are likely to need every day and often many times a day. Apart from the Special Vocabularies, few of the words in it will be unknown to the average student; what he will probably not know is the manner or variety of ways in which they are currently used.

Nor is it a dictionary of slang, which should never be learned from dictionaries. The great majority of words appearing in the following pages are perfectly good Spanish, though some of them are colloquial and would be avoided in literary Spanish in the same way as 'don't' or 'a lot of' or 'ghastly' would be avoided in written English. Occasionally I have included a word which, although somewhat slangy, is either extremely common or is not covered by any more formal word, but in such cases I have made the fact clear.

As will be seen, the main part of the book is the Spanish-English section. It is here that appropriate commentary is made on any given word, and the English-Spanish section at the end is not intended as more than a cross-reference index; it would be a waste of space to make the comments twice over.

In addition to these main sections, however, I have included special vocabularies on several subjects, mostly of everyday concern, e.g. Cars, Domestic and Office Appurtenances, Food, etc. Such vocabularies are not easily accessible in the average dictionary but they are often required in practice and may be of use to people who know no Spanish at all but who have to go to Spain—perhaps with their wives—in connection with their work or even as tourists. These vocabularies are given both ways round, i.e. Spanish-English and English-Spanish, but for the sake of completeness all the words are included in the main section where any necessary commentary will be found.

The section on Music is hardly of everyday concern. My reason for including it is simply that it is information which, so far as I am aware, does not exist in any other book and is likely to be of use to the English-speaking musician—conductor or soloist—who visits Spain professionally. Chance brought me into fairly close contact with musical affairs in Spain, and I thought it a pity not to put on record the rather exceptional knowledge I gained.

Other appendices such as Miscellaneous Notes, Falsos Amigos and the like are intended more for general study than for ready reference, indeed I hope that the whole book, as often as not; in fact in past participles it tends to disappear altogether. *Cambiado*, for example, becomes almost *cambiao* in rapid speech, and there is a story of a peasant who came to the big city and, in his over-anxiety to speak the best Castilian, referred to Bilbao as Bilbado.

Spaniards have an instinctive dislike of double consonants when one of these is 's'. It feels wrong to them for a word to begin with, say, 'sp', e.g. Spain, and they want to put an 'e' in front: España. When speaking English they will sometimes say 'an especial one' rather than 'a special one'. As for three consonants together, it gives them the horrors. The clot of consonants in the middle of a word like Sedgwick looks to them as some Polish or Czecho-Slovakian words do to us. Ask any Spaniard to pronounce 'crisps'; it is almost a physical impossibility. He will say 'creeps' or 'crísapas'. Spaniards like their words well ventilated. The sound 'ks' is almost equally repugnant to their instincts and the very letter 'x', although it exists in Spanish, is named *equis*. 'X' before consonants is like 's'; explosión— *esplosión*; between vowels, like soft 'gs': existir— *egsistir*, taxi— *tagsi.*

They are not fond of final consonants, especially in words of foreign origin, e.g. *coñac* (cognac), which they invariably pronounce *coñá*. It is true that they will accept the ones directed by their own language, i.e. words ending in J, L, N, R, S and Z, but a final 'd', although authoritative, tends to get ignored, e.g. Madrid (pron. *Madrí*), Usted (pron. *Usté*), and if a word ends with any other letter than those mentioned, so much the worse for the letter. Philip Morris cigarettes (which were widely sold on the black market), are called *Fili*; Dry Sack, originally bottled for the English market but now sold in Spain, is called *Drisa*.

Other sounds which the Spaniards shy away from are less easy to generalise about but there are several cases of the substitution of 'r' for 'l' and vice versa. These seem to have arisen simply through an unconscious desire to perfect the mouthability of a word coupled, perhaps, with an ignorance of, or indifference to, its origin, rather as we have corrupted the word 'baluster' into 'banister'. I list a few of them:

Word	Meaning	Expected	
Argel	Algiers	Alger	(cf. Shakespeare's 'Argier', *Tempest*, I, ii)
lirio	lily	lilio	(Lat. *lilium*, though Greek *leirion*)
milagro	miracle	miraglo	(Lat. *miraculum*)
peligro	danger	periglo	(Lat. *periculum*)
peluca	wig	peruca	(It. *parrucca* though Fr.-Lat. *pilus*; Span. *pelo*)
recluta	recruit	recruta	(Fr. *recroître*. It. also *recluta*)

Accent. There are virtually no class distinctions in Spanish accents. One is often asked by foreigners 'Where is the best English spoken?' and is obliged to reply that Standard English is for the most part a matter of class and has only the slightest regional variations. It is as astonishing for a Spaniard to discover that we can place an Englishman socially within a few seconds of his opening his mouth as it is for us to hear the poorest and humblest Spaniard speaking with a beauty and precision that anyone might be proud of. A Spaniard can be, and is, placed socially by other Spaniards but, in so far as this depends on his way of speaking, it will be his vocabulary rather than his accent which reveals him. Accent reveals regional variations, not social.

Diminutive. The diminutive hardly survives in Standard English, except in such cases as 'birdie' for 'bird', a use which we mostly retain for children, though it still exists in many parts of Scotland, e.g. 'a wee bittie of bread'. In Spanish it is still alive and kicking and apart from the direct meaning of 'little' (*cucharilla*=little spoon=tea-spoon; *platillo*=little plate=saucer, etc.), it tends above all to indicate an attitude of mind. It denotes friendliness, kindliness, or at all events a desire to seem pleasant or to put things pleasantly (as it does in the case of 'a wee bittie of bread'). If a telephonist says *Espere un momento* that is the straightforward 'Will you hang on a moment?': but if she says *Espere un momentito* she is being rather more cordial or polite about it and it would then equate with 'Would you mind waiting *one* moment?'

I remember once being stopped by a Civil Guard while driving in Spain. He examined my papers as a matter of routine and then, as so often in Spain, started a most

friendly conversation. He said *¡Muy solo va Usted! ¡Solito!*
In so far as this can be translated it would be something like
'You're a lonely traveller! All by yourself!' but what it
chiefly indicated was a friendly sympathy at my having to
travel such long distances all alone. On another occasion I
gave a man a lift and as we were descending a series of hair-
pin bends he made some reference to *las curvitas estas*. It
was a form of understatement, as they were very sharp
curves, but in actual fact he was a trifle nervous of them
and was really suggesting to me, as nicely as he could,
that I should take them gently. On quite a different
occasion I patronised rather a *cursi* shop which had a most
obsequious girl behind the counter. When she had produced what I wanted she said *¿Una cosita más?* This
is not an uncommon expression in a shop; I mention it
chiefly to point out that the diminutive may be used for in-
gratiation and that the implied friendliness is not necessarily
genuine.

In other cases the diminutive is a useful way of dealing
with such words as 'rather', 'somewhat', 'quite', and the
suffix '-ish': *tempranito* = 'rather early', 'earlyish'; *cerquita* =
'quite near', 'not very far'. And there is one very common
double diminutive which you should know, viz. *chiquitito*,
the double diminutive of *chico*, which means 'teeny-weeny',
though it is widely used and not merely addressed to children;
'minute' (adj.) would be another translation of it. In general,
however, the diminutive cannot be taught in any cut-and-
dried manner; you must simply make yourself aware that
when friendliness or understatement are required it may be
a solution of your difficulties.

Superlative. By this I mean, of course, the suffix
. . . *ísimo* (note that the 's' is single in Spanish). It is very
useful to remember when you are translating 'frightfully',
'tremendously', etc., followed by a simple adjective, e.g. *¡es
listísimo!* 'He's *fright*fully clever!'; *¡es Usted amabilísimo!*
'You're *terr*ibly kind!' It really is the extreme and not to
be used lightly. *Muy, muy amable* is already very cordial;
and it is absolute, not comparative, i.e. you cannot say
la persona fortísima to mean 'the strongest person', you
must say *la persona más fuerte*.

Imperative. Spaniards use the Imperative a great deal more freely than we do and it is not considered rude. Under Diminutives, above, I instanced *Espere un momento* as being the straightforward way of saying 'Will you hang on a moment?' but it is nevertheless a direct imperative and the literal translation—'Hang on a moment' or 'Wait a moment' would be very abrupt for us. Most of our polite phrases are in the form of a question, e.g. 'Would you be kind enough to…?' or even just plain 'Will you?' *¿Quiere?* is not uncommon in Spanish, e.g. *¿Quiere ayudarme con esto?* 'Will you give me a hand with this?' (or rather 'can you', since it is polite to assume they would if they could), but this form is really rather more familiar. The formal Spanish phrase for 'Would you be good enough to' is *Haga el favor de*, again an imperative whose literal translation 'Have the goodness to', although also formal, strikes us as distinctly frigid. See also the entry under **oiga**.

Slang. In the following pages I have instanced an occasional word as slangy. I should perhaps mention that Spaniards, on the whole, use less slang than we do, indeed they play about with words a good deal less altogether and are not very adventurous in exploiting perfectly good words which already exist in their own language. The English translations I have given are therefore often a good deal more slangy than the Spanish equivalents opposite them.

I have often asked a Spaniard 'Don't you have a word (say) *portentoso?*'(portentous), only to get the reply 'Ah yes, we have it but we don't use it'. The British, or at all events the more educated of them, seem to me to exploit their own language a good deal more fully and rather enjoy bringing in an unusual word. We are also, at all levels of education, rather fond of coining words at a moment's notice. Amongst my English friends in Madrid our daily beverages at the *quiosco* on the corner were vermouth and beer and when it was our round we were likely to say 'Are you vermouthing or beering?' When we tried this on a Spanish friend, however, saying '*¿Quieres vermutar o cervezar?*', not only did we not raise a glimmer of a smile (though Spaniards have an excellent sense of humour) but we were seriously told that you could not say such things in Spanish. Perhaps this was an extreme case. Students in all countries enjoy using unorthodox words but on the whole Spaniards are orthodox and, as I say, unadventurous. This may perhaps be of some comfort to you.

SPANISH—ENGLISH

A

absoluto, en. This is misleading because you tend tó think it means 'absolutely' whereas it really means 'absolutely *not*', i.e. 'not in the slightest', 'haven't a clue', etc. A context I remember is: Q. *¿Sabes nadar?* A. *En absoluto.* Q. 'Can you swim?' A. 'Not a stroke'. A friend of mine once got it in reply to the question: *¿Sabe Vd. donde vive el Señor. . . ?* and was led to believe that it was the name of a street or district in Madrid. It is not necessarily colloquial. If you really mean 'absolutely' you say *absolutamente* or *por completo* (q.v.).

aburrido. Yes, this does mean 'bored', but the illogical part is that it also means 'boring': *¡Qué película más aburrida!* 'What a boring film!' and *¡Qué aburrido!* 'What a bore!', 'How boring!' Similar considerations also apply to *divertido* (q.v.).

acaso. *Por si acaso*, 'Just in case', 'If by any chance'. *Los guardaré por si acaso*, 'I'll keep them just in case'. It is a cliché and worth learning off pat. Surprisingly enough it does not take the subjunctive: *Por si acaso viene el Señor Tal*, 'If by any chance Mr. So-and-So should come'. You may, however, omit the *acaso* in which case you do use the subjunctive: *Por si viniera*, 'In case he comes'.

accidente (m). Accident (*v.* CARS).

aceite (m). It is one of the disconcerting things about Spanish that although the Latin word for 'oil' is used, in some form, in practically all European languages, including English and German, Spanish itself, perhaps the most Latin language of the lot, uses an Arabic word. The same applies to 'olives', which are called *aceitunas*, though *olivas* is used for the trees on which they grow.

Strictly speaking *aceite* means 'olive oil' and it will be assumed that this is meant unless the context suggests another sort but, given an appropriate context, it may mean any sort of oil you please. It is included here chiefly for the benefit of car users since, in a car context, it means lubricating oil.

acelerador (m). Accelerator (*v.* CARS). Easy! but note that it has only one 'c'.

acento (m). 'Accent' in nearly all senses (*v.* MUSIC).

acorde (m). Chord (*v.* MUSIC).

actual. A false friend. As in French, it means 'present', e.g. *las circunstancias actuales*, 'the present circumstances', *actualmente*, 'at the present time'; *actualidades*, 'current events'. In so far as 'actually' can be translated it would be something like *en realidad* but we tend to use it in contexts where the Spaniards would have no equivalent.

acuerdo (m). Agreement (Fr. *accord*) and *De acuerdo*, 'I agree' or 'Agreed' (Fr. *d'accord*). The full expression is, of course, *estar de acuerdo con . . . en . . .*, 'to be in agreement with . . . about. . . '. See also **conforme**, which is perhaps even commoner.

¡adelante! Basically 'forward' but the proper expression for 'Come in!' when anyone knocks at your door, so you may need it in your hotel. If you prefer a shorter word you may say *¡pase!* but *¡adelante!* is better. Another meaning is 'Off we go!' or 'Off you go!' (Fr. *en route*) though for 'Off we go' *¡Vámonos!* is more common.

Delante, as you no doubt know, means 'in front of'; I mention it here merely to warn you against the temptation of saying *en frente de* which means 'opposite'.

además. You probably know perfectly well that this means 'moreover', 'besides', etc., and you may have no difficulty in understanding it when it is said to you, but you may have difficulty in remembering to use it yourself so I commend it to your attention. It is extremely common and often used in conversation to tack two sentences together where we should not bother, . . . *y además . . .*, '. . . and another thing . . .', 'what's more', etc.

¡adiós! This, as the merest child knows, is the universal word for 'good-bye', but at the end of the average conversation it is likely to be coupled with other words. The exclamation marks are here included to denote a special use of it in Spanish which we do not have in English, viz. when greeting a person *en passant*, on occasions when we should say 'Hello!' Spaniards who imagine they know English, frequently say 'Good-bye!' thus sounding almost rude. We seem conscious of the meeting aspect of such encounters and the Spaniards of the parting, though of course the real meaning of 'go with God' is the root of the matter. Certainly its use at such a moment suggests strongly that there is no question of stopping to exchange a word but it nevertheless has the effect of a greeting. My hall-porter says it to me as I pass him in the doorway.

For a more detailed examination of 'good-bye' problems see under **hasta**.

ahumado. Smoked (*v.* FOOD).

aire (m). Choke (*v.* CARS). It also applies to the air in the tires. *Dar aire*, 'to pump' (air into the tires).

ajo (m). Garlic (*v.* FOOD).

al . . . (inf). e.g. *al llegar, al comprarlo*, etc. This is one of the commonest ways of rendering 'when' in Spanish and it is not necessarily colloquial. *Al llegar* might well be translated 'on arrival' or 'when arriving' but we are more likely to say 'when you (he, it, etc.) get (got) there' as we tend to avoid impersonal usages in colloquial speech and use the pronoun 'you' very freely, e.g. *Al comprar un reloj*, 'When you buy a watch'. When a specific person is being mentioned then *cuando* (usually with the subjunctive) is needed, e.g. 'When Pepe comes', *Cuando venga Pepe*, though it would be just possible to say *Al llegar Pepe*. If, however, the 'when' is a question meaning 'at what time' then *cuando* with the indicative is necessary, e.g. 'When you buy the ticket you should ask when the bus leaves', *Al comprar el billete hay que preguntar cuándo sale el autobús*.

A useful cliché is *al parecer*, 'evidently', 'apparently'.

albaricoque (m). Apricot (*v.* FOOD). The word is of Arabic origin. cf. also 16th century 'apricocks'.

alcantarilla (f). Sewer, town drains. It is normally used in the plural.

aleta (f) Fender, mudguard (*v.* CARS).

alfombra (f). Carpet, rug (*v.* DOM. APP.).

allí, allá. Both words mean 'there', as you know, and it is virtually impossible to distinguish between them. Two points, however, may be noted: 1. Spaniards often omit the word altogether after the verb *estar* when the place is too obvious to need specification, e.g. on the telephone: Q. 'Is So-and-So there?' A. 'No, he's not here'. Q. *¿Está Fulano?* A. *No, no está.* 2. *Más allá* is a cliché for 'further on'. Q. 'Is it here?' A. 'No, further on'. Q. *¿Es aquí?* A. *No, más allá*.

Allá is not so specific in denoting distance as *allí*, and there are many instances in which it must be used instead; *tan allá*, 'as far'; *más allá*, 'in the next world'; *muy allá*, 'far away'. It is also employed before place names to indicate 'distance': *allá en Rusia*, 'away in Russia'; *allá en América*, 'over there in America'. When preceding 'time', it denotes the past; *allá en tiempo de los godos*, 'long ago in the time of the Goths'.

almendra (f). Almond (*v.* FOOD). A favourite *aperitivo* (*q.v.*).

almirez (m). Mortar, i.e. of pestle and mortar. It is not uncommon in Spanish kitchens (*v.* DOM. APP.).

almohada (f). Pillow, cushion (*v.* DOM. APP.).

alquilar, -er (m). *Alquilar* is the verb and means 'to rent', 'to hire'. *Alquiler* is the noun and means the 'rent'. *Alquiler sin chófer*, 'drive- yourself '.

alrededor. Round about, thereabouts (Fr. *environ*). *Alrededor de las ocho*, 'About eight o'clock'; *Le espero alrededor del 15 de junio*, 'I expect him round about the 15th June'.

alto. 'High', as you know, but here included for musicians: in a musical context it is likely to mean 'sharp'. N.B. It cannot be used to mean 'contralto', as it frequently is in English (*v.* MUSIC).

amable. Perhaps hardly worth mentioning but it is so common, especially in polite conversation, that it should be kept at the tongue's tip: *Es Vd. muy amable*, 'It's awfully kind of you'; *¿Sería Vd. tan amable de darme sus señas?* 'Would you be good enough to give me your address?'

ambiente (m). 'Atmosphere' in the metaphorical sense, and extremely common. 'Surroundings' might often be the translation. *No puede trabajar en este ambiente*, 'You (or he) can't work in such an atmosphere' (surroundings); *El ambiente no es muy apropiado para el estudio*, 'The atmosphere (or climate of opinion) is not very conducive to study'; *Ese café tiene un ambiente muy agradable (simpático)*, 'That café has a nice atmosphere'.

amortiguador (m). Shock-absorber (*v.* CARS).

anchoa (f). Anchovy (*v.* FOOD).

andar, ¡anda! *Andar* means 'to go' in the sense of 'to walk' and every schoolgirl knows that *andante* in music means 'walking', i.e. neither running nor crawling but at an ordinary, prosaic pace. If you ask why I bother to mention it I reply with a counter-question: how do you translate 'He came on foot'? The answer is usually *Vino andando*. If you mean 'walk' in the sense of 'to go for a walk' then a better verb is *pasear* (no doubt you are fully conscious of the evening *paseo* which is a feature of every town and village in Spain). *Andaba por la calle* means 'He was walking down the street'.

 ¡Anda! is a very common exclamation, similar to *¡Vaya!* (*q.v.*). Whereas *¡Vaya!* contains a notion of disbelief or incredulity, however *¡Anda!* has more the feeling of encouragement or admiration. If, for example, someone is being persuaded to sing, or tell a funny story or perform some other act of heroism then the ejaculation *¡Anda!* has the force of 'Come on! Let's hear you'. In such cases it is usually followed by another phrase: *¡Anda, hombre! No te hagas de rogar.* 'Come on, boy. Don't be shy!' (Lit., 'Don't make us insist'). If, however, you are serving at table-tennis and you fluff the service, particularly if you fluff it twice in succession, then the onlookers may well exclaim *¡Anda!* as conveying 'Come on! Get on with it!' or even 'For heaven's sake'.[1] There is, however, no real English equivalent as on such occasions we tend to become a little tight-lipped and deliberately say nothing whereas the more articulate and vocal Latins have a word for all occasions. I think the best phrase to bear in mind is simply 'Come on!'

[1] You yourself are likely to exclaim *¡Vaya!* indicating impatient disgust.

It should be noted that Spaniards often drag the second *a* fairly heavily although the accent is technically on the first. Whether this is done or not depends on whether it is the encouraging or the facetious aspect you wish to stress; if it is encouragement the first syllable is accented in the proper way and the word is said with animation, being the approximate equivalent of 'Go it!' or 'Come on!' If somebody suddenly does something surprisingly clever, such as juggling with oranges, and the bystanders' reaction is a mixture of admiration and irony then something like *¡Anda, qué listo!* is to be expected. (My! Isn't he clever!') and here the second syllable is accented a little more heavily. If, however, he does something rather stupid, such as knocking over somebody's drink and the reaction is therefore more derisive, then a likely exclamation is *¡Andá! ¡Pues la has hecho buena!* ('You're a beauty!') and then the *Anda* is said more slowly and the second syllable may be dragged out enormously.

anguila, angula (f). *Anguila*, eel. One of the commonest forms in which they are eaten is whilst still at the recently hatched stage when they are fried in bulk and look like so much spaghetti. In this form they are referred to as *angulas*.

anillo (m). Any sort of small 'ring' including that worn on the hand.

anoche. I mention this merely to remind you that it means 'last night' and not 'to-night', as one may all too readily tend to feel.[1] 'To-night', *esta noche.*

apagar. To switch off (*v.* DOM. APP.).

aparcar. The usual word for 'to park', though *estacionar* is also used.

aperitivos (m). Something of a Falso Amigo since to us it spells drinks whereas to a Spaniard it spells eats, i.e. the little snacks that usually accompany drinks in Spain. You may very well be asked, when you have just ordered a *combinación* (i.e. a gin-and-It) *¿Quiere aperitivos?* or *¿Algo de aperitivo?* and be rather disconcerted in consequence, but the question really means, 'Do you want anything to eat with it?' e.g. almonds, olives, crisps, prawns, anchovies, little cubes of cheese, etc. Quite often you will be given *aperitivos* without being asked. Another, more colloquial word for it is *tapas* (*q.v.*).

apio (m). Celery (*v.* FOOD).

apostar. To stake, i.e. at cards (*v.* CARDS). It also means 'to bet' at a race-course and *¿Cuánto te apuestas?* 'How much d'you bet?' and *Te apuesto*, 'I bet you' are common clichés apart from the course.

[1] Classical scholars may be interested in the origin: it is a corruption of the Latin *ad noctem.*

apreciable. Something of a Falso Amigo; it is more absolute and less comparative in Spanish and so means 'valuable' or 'respectable' rather than 'appreciable'—*Esto es una contribución apreciable a nuestra biblioteca,* 'This is a valuable contribution to our library'.

The difference shows up rather more clearly with *inapreciable,* which means 'invaluable'; *Esta información es inapreciable,* 'This information is invaluable', which is very different from 'inappreciable'. In Spanish the thing is too great to be valued, in English too small.

Apreciado Señor is a common opening to a letter and equates approximately with 'Dear Mr. So-and-So'. (In this context it is interchangeable with *Estimado.*) (*v.* comprehensive note under **querer.**)

aprovechar. A perfectly proper word and not colloquial as such but frequently used in speech and worth bearing in mind as we have no single word which covers it. It means literally 'to take advantage of', 'to exploit', 'to take the opportunity of trying', 'to make the most of'. Quite often our word would be simply 'to use': *Pues ya que lo hemos comprado hay que aprovecharlo,* 'Well now we've bought it we shall have to use it'. *Aproveche bien la oportunidad,* 'Make the most of the chance'.

Que le aproveche (or *Buen provecho*) is the conventional response when you have discovered somebody in the act of eating and they have conventionally invited you to share the meal by saying: *¿Vd. gusta?* You should be aware of this pleasant and delicate convention which applies between complete strangers and requires both the offer and the declining of the offer. Do not be surprised if a humble-looking man in the train appears to offer you his lunch and on the other hand do not accept it nor decline with a *No, gracias*; decline simply with a *Buen provecho* (or *Que le aproveche*). Sometimes, of course, the offer may be genuine and may be accepted, but then the context of conversation will make the fact clear.

apuntar. To jot down, to make a note of, to prompt (i.e. in a theatre), to aim at (i.e. on a shooting-range or in warfare): *Voy a apuntar los números,* 'I'll just jot down the numbers'; *¿Quiere apuntar sus señas?* 'Do you want to make a note of his address?'; *Apuntó cuidadosamente al blanco* (*a la diana*), 'He took careful aim at the target (bull's-eye)'. It will be seen, therefore, that it is a Falso Amigo; To appoint, *nombrar.*

arandela (f). Washer, e.g. of a tap or screw (*v.* DOM. APP.).

árbol (de levas). Camshaft (*v.* CARS).

archivo, etc. The basic word for 'file' from which *un archivo,* 'a filing-room'; *los archivos,* 'the files' (in a general sense; an individual file is *una carpeta*); *archivar,* 'to file'; *archivador,* 'filing-cabinet'; *archivero, -a,* 'filing-clerk' (*v.* OFF. APP.).

arenque (m). Herring (*v.* FOOD).

arpa (f). Harp (*v.* MUSIC). Although feminine you say *el arpa* in the singular.

arrancar, arranque (m). 'To start up' and 'self-starter', respectively (*v.* CARS).

arreglar. Aɴ extremely common verb meaning to arrange, to put right, to settle, 'to fix'.[1] *Está arreglado*, 'It's O.K.', 'It's all arranged', 'I've fixed it', etc. *Voy a arreglarlo*, 'I'll go and fix it up', 'I'm going to settle it'; *¿Puede arreglarme esto?* 'Can you put this right for me?'
  Un arreglo is the straightforward noun for 'an arrangement' whether it be a business one, a private one, or a musical one. It is a very useful word.

arroz (m). Rice (*v.* FOOD).

as (m). Ace (*v.* CARDS).

asado (m). Roast, baked (*v.* FOOD).

asco (*v.* asqueroso).

así. Means 'thus', 'of course' (Fr. *ainsi*), but how often do you use the word 'thus' in English? 'Like' is more like it. *Así era*, 'It was like that', 'That's how it was'; *Algo así*, 'Something like that', 'Something of that sort'. *Así*, 'Like this', 'Like that'. *Así, así*, with an appropriate motion of the hands, is 'so, so' (Fr. *comme-ci comme-ça*) and in fact a gesture is a common accompaniment to the word.[2] 'About six o'clock' could strictly be translated: *Alrededor de las seis* (Fr. *environ (vers) six heures*) but in practice it is quite likely to be *A las seis o así*; 'or thereabouts', *o así*. It is so common that it would be next to impossible to give examples of all its uses, but if you keep it in the forefront of your mind it should not take you long to find them out. Bear in mind, too, that it is not normally the translation of the English 'so' in such phrases as 'I think so' or 'I told him so', i.e. *Creo que sí*, and *Se lo dije*, respectively; but if you meant 'That's what I told him', i.e. paying a particular attention to what was told, then you would say *Así se lo dije*.

asiento (m). Seat (*v.* CARS)

asistir.—A Falso Amigo; like the French it means 'to be present at': *Asistí a la ceremonia*, 'I was present at the ceremony' (and with no suggestion of taking part; merely watching). *¿Había muchos asistentes?* 'Were there many people present?' 'To assist' is *ayudar*.

asperón (m). A sort of sand for cleaning floors (*v.* DOM. APP.).

---

[1] I might have added 'to regulate', but this is properly handled by *regular* (*q.v.*).
[2] 'As long as that' would be *así de largo*, indicating how long.

asqueroso, asco. These, in colloquial usage, border on slang and I do not commend them specially to your attention. There are undoubtedly moments, however, when one earnestly wishes to describe something as 'filthy', 'vile', 'ghastly', 'appalling', and *asqueroso* is no more slangy than are any of these words in English. It is strong without being indecent or vulgar—but don't overdo it. *Asco* is the noun and *asqueroso* the adjective. ¡*Qué asco!*, 'How revolting!', i.e. lit. 'What a horror'; ¡*Qué horror!* is a milder version of the same thing.

atender. An Unreliable Friend: it means 'to attend' only in the sense of 'to pay attention' (e.g. 'attend to what I say'), not in the sense of 'to be present at', which is *asistir* (another False Friend *q.v.*).

atún (m). Tuna fish (*v.* FOOD). A very decent second-best to salmon.

auricular (m). The earpiece, e.g. of a telephone.

auto (m). Abbreviation for car (*v.* CARS).

ave (f) (*el ave* in the singular). Lit. 'bird', but used in the general sense for 'poultry' (*v.* FOOD).

avellana (f). Hazel-nut (*v.* FOOD).

avería (f). Breakdown, whether it be of a car or the electric light (or other things) and all too frequently needed; not, however, a nervous breakdown, which would be *crisis nerviosa*. There is nothing in the least colloquial about this word.

azulejo (m). Tile, of the sort used for floors and walls; it suggests glazed tiles and would not be used for roofs, for which the word is *tejas* (*v.* DOM. APP.).

B

bajo. In the normal way, as you know, it means 'low', but in a musical context it will probably mean 'bass', i.e. in a choir, or 'flat'. 'A low note' is *Una nota grave*, though 'It's a bit low for me', *Es un poco bajo para mí* (*v.* MUSIC).

ballesta (f). Spring, of the laminated type (*v.* CARS) (for the spiral sort *v.* **muelle**).

banca (f). Bank, at CARDS (*q.v.*). N.B. In this context it is feminine whereas the public institution is masculine, e.g. *Banco de España.*[1] The word *banquero* might be used for 'banker' in cards, but it is more usual to hear ¿*Quién tiene la banca?* for 'Who's banker?'

bandeja (f). Tray (*v.* both DOM. and OFF. APP.).

---

[1] *Banca* is also used to refer to 'banking' in general.

baño (m). Both 'a bath' (i.e. what you take) and 'the bath' (i.e. the thing you take it in) (*v*. DOM. APP.).

baraja (f). A pack of cards (*v*. CARDS). **barajar.** To shuffle, to make. Spanish playing-cards are different from those used in the rest of Western Europe (*v*. Note to PLAYING-CARDS, p. 141).

barbaridad (f). Lit., of course, a 'barbarity', but colloquially it is widely used where we should probably say 'awful'. *¡Qué barbaridad!* 'How awful', 'How disgusting', 'How maddening'. It is the normal way of expressing sympathetic indignation if someone tells you of a misfortune and one equation is the noise 'st . . . st . . . st' (i.e. clucking with the teeth. N.B., however, that this noise is a Falso Amigo as in Spanish it signifies a negative and equates with 'Good gracious, no!')

A common use of *barbaridad* is in the phrase *una barbaridad de*, 'an awful lot'; *Tuve una barbaridad de cosas que hacer*, 'I had an awful lot of things to do', or *Había una barbaridad de gente*, 'There was a fearful crowd'.[1] 'Awful' is probably the best word to connect it with, since in both languages the word can be used very mildly, though originally it was strong. It cannot, however, mean 'awfully' in the good sense, e.g. 'It's awfully kind of you', for which the translation would have to be simply *Vd. es muy, muy amable*.

barítono. Baritone.

barra (f). This means 'bar' in almost every sense except the sort you drink at. It is the name given to a 'stroke' in typing (i.e. a downward stroke /, not a horizontal one which would be *guión*) (*v*. OFF. APP.). It is also applied to a 'small loaf of bread'—one might say a 'large roll'—and the cry *¡Hay barras!* is a frequent street-cry in Spain.

In Music *barra*, 'bar-line' (not the bar itself, which is *compás*, *q.v.*). *Las barras*, 'the double bar'. *Desde las barras*, 'From the double bar' (*v*. MUSIC).

bastos (m). This may be translated 'clubs' in cards provided it is understood that it applies only to Spanish packs (*v*. Note, p. 141). 'Clubs' as we know them are *tréboles*.

batería (f). Battery (*v*. CARS).

batín (m). Dressing-gown.

batuta (f). Baton, of the conductor's sort (*v*. MUSIC).

baúl (m). A trunk, of the type you pack things in.

bayeta (f). Floor-cloth (*v*. DOM. APP.).

baza (f). Trick, in cards (*v*. CARDS).

bemol (m). Flat, in the musical sense, i.e. ♭ (*v*. MUSIC).

[1] Another common way of putting this is with *montón*. *Tuve un montón de cosas que hacer.*

berengena (f). Eggplant (*v.* FOOD).

bidé (m). Bidet, taken from the French, as it is in English (*v.* DOM. APP.).

biela (f). Connecting-rod (*v.* CARS).

bizcocho (m). A False Friend, though perhaps not a very important one; it does not mean 'biscuit', it means 'sponge-cake'. 'A biscuit' is *una galleta*.

blanca (f). Minim (cf. Fr. *une blanche*) (*v.* MUSIC).

bloque (m). Block, here more especially 'cylinder block' (*v.* CARS). It is *not* used for blocks of buildings, e.g. 'three blocks ahead', for which the proper word is *manzana* (*q.v.*).

bobina (f). Usually 'spool' but here more particularly 'transformer' (*v.* CARS).

bocacalle (f). Lit. 'street-mouth' and used where we should say ' corner'. You are likely to get it when asking the way, e.g. *La tercera bocacalle a la izquierda*, 'The third corner on the left'. As with so many words that are easy to understand, it is less easy to remember, in time, to use it.

bocina (f). Horn of a car; it suggests rather the old-fashioned, honking sort but nevertheless a good deal used, though *claxon* is better (*v.* CARS).

bollo (m). A roll of bread.

bolso (m). Handbag, usually of the sort carried by ladies, though it can also apply to a double-handled suitcase. A very small handbag might be called a *bolsillo*, though this normally means 'pocket'.

bomba (f). One has no difficulty in remembering that this means a 'bomb' but it is a little disconcerting to realise that it also means 'pump' in every sense, whether hand-pump, foot-pump or gas pump (*v.* CARS).

bombilla (f). Electric bulb (*v.* DOM APP.). *Lámpara* may also be used.

bonito (m) (noun). A kind of fish, rather like tuna fish, i.e. slightly brown in colour. It is a favourite for canning, and when tinned is usually called *escabeche* (*q.v.*), which is really the name given to the manner of preparing it.

bonito, -a (adj). This is almost as common as 'nice' in English and in an immense number of contexts the words equate: *¡Qué bonito!* 'How nice', 'Isn't that nice!' Q. *¿Qué tal la película?* A. *Muy bonita.* Q. 'What was the film like?' A. 'Very nice'. When applied to persons, however, it tends to concern appearances rather than qualities. If we say in English 'She is a very nice girl', we are usually thinking of her nature, whereas if a Spaniard says *Es una chica muy bonita*, he is thinking of her face and the translation is 'pretty'.[1] To describe her nature he would say *muy simpática, muy buena*.[2] *Bonito* is, of course, the diminutive of *bueno* and the remarks on page 12 are germane.

boquerones (m. pl.). Small fish, similar to whitebait. They are anchovies but, although usually tinned, the flesh is white. They are flavoured with vinegar and garlic and are a favourite *aperitivo*.

bote (m). A tin (Amer., can) of meat or other preserved food, etc. Another word for it is *lata* (*q.v.*) and it is a little difficult to distinguish between them. Generally speaking a *lata* suggests a larger tin than a *bote*, but on the other hand a *bote* suggests a round tin whereas a *lata* suggests a square one (e.g. corned beef). You need not bother much about the difference; either will do.

botones. A buttons, i.e. a messenger-boy. It has a delightfully Victorian sound to our ears, but then one of the pleasures of visiting Spain is to recapture in the twentieth century some savour of the nineteenth. Any business firm or other organisation has at least one *botones* who may be ordered about on all manner of errands without any compunction and they are not all 'boys'; many of them are grown men. The word *muchacho* may also be used and again is not literally a 'boy'.

bragas (f. pl.). Panties. *Calzarse las bragas*, 'to wear the trousers'.

broma (f). A joke, but rather more of the practical sort; a joke, in the sense of a funny story is *un chiste* (*q.v.*): *Era una broma*, 'It was all a joke'; *Lo hizo en broma*, 'He did it for fun'; *¿En serio o en broma?* 'D'you mean it seriously or are you joking?' Obviously other translations would be 'lark', 'prank', etc.
 Una broma pesada, 'A poor sort of joke' (of the practical sort).
 Una broma de mal gusto, 'A joke in poor taste'.
 No estoy para bromas, 'I'm in dead earnest'.

bronce (m). Brass (*v.* MUSIC); bronze, etc.

bujía (f). Spark plug (*v.* CARS).

bulón (m). Spring pin.

buró (m). This is the Spanish spelling of 'bureau' and means a 'roll-top desk' (*v.* OFF. APP.).

butaca (f). Arm-chair (*v.* DOM. APP.). It also means a stall in the theatre.

---

[1] Though a more usual, and perhaps stronger, word for pretty is *guapa*.
[2] *Buena* in this case tends to suggest that she is plain-looking; cf. Amer. 'homely'.

C

caballo (m). Lit. horse, as you know, but in Spanish playing-cards it is a 'Knight' and comes between the Knave and the King, being thus equivalent to Queen (v. Note, p. 141).

caber. This curious word is extremely common but hard to remember to use, since we have no equivalent verb in English. Your grammar-books will no doubt have told you that it means 'to have room for', 'to fit in', 'to allow', but in practice it is more often used in the negative or interrogative than in the positive. It is an everyday occurrence to hear a taxi-driver say *No caben más que cuatro*, 'There is only room for four' (and how right he is!) or for anyone to say *No cabe duda*, 'There's no doubt about it', 'Certainly', 'Undoubtedly'. If the Mad Hatter's Tea Party had taken place in Spain, Alice, on her arrival, would probably have been greeted with cries of *¡No cabe! ¡No cabe!*[1] If, however, a Spaniard is trying to fit a last piece of luggage into the boot of a car and finds, to his satisfaction, that it will go in, he may well say *¡Sí! Cabe*, 'Yes, it'll go', 'It fits', 'There's room', etc. You may find useful a device for remembering to use it which was employed by a friend of mine; it is absurd and illogical but mnemonics of this sort often are, though they serve: her taxi experience with *No caben más que cuatro* always made her think of 'cribbed', '*cabin'd*' and 'confined' as indeed one so frequently is in Madrid taxis, and the root word was 'cabin'. A more logical concept might be 'fit' but this is usually better translated by *conviene* (v. **convenir**).

It is, of course, a highly irregular verb. You might hear a Spaniard hoping to enter an already full car, say *¿Quepo yo?* 'Is there room for me?' without realising that *quepo* is the first person singular of this same verb. I suggest you look up its conjugation before embarking on it, though *No cabe duda* should be learnt off pat.

cacahuete (m). Peanut (v. FOOD).

cacerola (f). Saucepan of a flat, open type (v. DOM. APP.).

cadena (f). Chain (v. CARS).

cafetera (f). Lit. coffee-pot, but sometimes used for a 'kettle' if you bring one with you; the Spaniards do not use kettles in the ordinary way (v. DOM. APP., also **tetera**).

caigo. Lit. 'I fall'. It borders on slang but no other expression quite fits and it is not in much danger of abuse by the indiscriminate. It means '*I see*' in the sense that the blind man used it (Amer. 'I get it'), i.e. the penny drops, you suddenly

---

[1] See also Footnote 1 under **como**.

tumble to it. A milder and less slangy expression on such an occasion is ¡ *Ya, ya, ya!* but there is nothing at all vulgar about *caigo*.

caja (f). As you know, it means 'box' and *caja de cambio*, 'gear-box' (*v.* CARS).

It equates with the French *caisse* and German *Kasse* and therefore also means 'cash-desk'; so that *cajero* means 'cashier', and *caja fuerte* 'safe', 'strong-box' (*v.* OFF. APP.).[1]

calabacín (m). Marrow (i.e. the vegetable; usually smaller than ours), one of the ingredients of *pisto* (*v.* FOOD).

calamares (m). Squids, a very Mediterranean dish, and a very nice one. They are either served fried or *en su tinta*, i.e. their own jet-black secretion (*v.* FOOD, also **chipirones**).

calcetines (m. pl.). Socks.

calderón (m). 'Pause', i.e. ⌒ (*v.* MUSIC).

caldo (m). The usual word for 'thin soup', consommé (*v.* FOOD).

callarse. This is a perfectly proper expression meaning 'to keep silent', 'to hold one's tongue'; it is only when used in the imperative that it tends to sound rude. *Cálle(n)se, por favor*, 'Will you kindly keep quiet?' although formally expressed, is comparatively strong language in both languages. *Cállate* is the ordinary Spanish for 'Shut up', 'Hold your tongue'. If you want to pray silence in a polite way you must use the expression '*guardar silencio*'.

calzoncillos (m. pl.). Pants, in English; Underpants, in American usage.

cama (f). Bed (*v.* DOM. APP.).

cámara (f). Lit. chamber (cf. 'heard in camera') but included here as it is the routine word for an inner-tube (*v.* CARS); photographic camera, etc.

camisa (f). Shirt but also 'sleeve' in engineering, e.g. 'cylinder-sleeve' (*v.* CARS). **camiseta,** undershirt.

cangrejo (m). Crab (*v.* FOOD). **cangrejo de río,** crayfish or crawfish.

cañería (f). Drain (*v.* DOM. APP.). *La cañería está atrancada*, 'The drain is blocked up'.

capot (m). Hood (*v.* CARS). Like many Spanish 'car' words it is taken over from the French.

cara de, tener. 'To look as if', 'to have the appearance of' (cf. Fr. *avoir l'air de*). Grammar-book, perhaps, but worth bearing in mind. *Tiene cara de haberse pasado la noche de juerga*, 'He looks as though he'd spent a night on the tiles'.

Cara also means the side of a gramophone record.

---

[1] *Caja de ahorros*, Fr. *caisse d'épargne*, Ger. *Sparkasse*, 'Savings-bank'.

caracoles (m). Snails (v. FOOD). They are less common than in France.

caradura (m and f). Lit. 'hard face' and meaning a brazenly un-scrupulous person, a 'tough egg' who knows what he wants and is not over-fussy about the means of getting it. Normally it is masculine, though if it were applied to a woman she would be *una caradura*. 'Brazen' is perhaps the best basic concept and the word *caradura* can be used in a general sense, i.e. meaning 'brazenness', as well as meaning the person possess-ing such qualities: e.g. *Este tío tiene una caradura imponente*, 'That fellow's got the cheek of the devil': *¡Qué cara más dura!*, 'What nerve!'

carburador (m). Carburetor (v. CARS).

cariño, cariñoso. *Cariño* is a diminutive of *caro* and, used to a person of the opposite sex, means 'darling', 'honey', 'sweet-heart', etc. In the general sense it means 'affection': *Le tenía mucho cariño*, 'I was very fond of her', 'I had much affection for her'.

Cariñoso, correspondingly, means 'kindly', 'affectionate', 'loving', and is often another word for 'nice': *Fué muy cariñoso conmigo*, 'He was awfully nice to me'. It also de-scribes the look people wear when they are in love, so I suppose one translation is 'starry-eyed'.

carne (f). The general word for meat as well as flesh (v. FOOD).

carpeta (f). This might be classed as a Falso Amigo as it has nothing whatever to do with 'carpet' for which the Spanish, as you know, is an Arab word: *alfombra*. *Carpeta* means 'file' of the sort used in offices (not the engineering sort, which is *lima*) though 'the files' in general are referred to as *los archivos* (v. OFF. APP.).

carrera (f). It means 'career' and 'race-course' but also 'ladder', of a stocking (v. DOM. APP.).

carta (f). Something of a False Friend as its most common mean-ing is 'letter' and not 'card'. 'Card' is normally *tarjeta*. There are occasions, however, when *carta* does mean 'card', e.g. in connection with playing-cards: *jugar a las cartas*, 'to play cards'. The original Spanish word for playing-cards was *naipes* but this is becoming obsolete.

cárter (m). This means 'crankcase', but do not ask me why. I imagine it was the make of an early model (v. CARS).

cartera (f). 'Letter-case' but applied both to the wallet in which a man carries his money and to the brief-case or attaché-case in which he carries papers, etc.

caso (m). A somewhat Unreliable Friend: in many contexts it equates well enough with 'case', e.g. *En este caso*, 'in that case'; *en todo caso*, 'in every case'; but in many others the translation

should be 'point', e.g. *vamos al caso*, 'let's get to the point';
el caso es que . . ., 'the point is . . .', 'the trouble is . . .', 'the
thing is . . .'. *Están muy bien pero el caso es que no puedo pagar
tanto*, 'They're very nice but the trouble is I can't afford
them'. Certain cases will lead you astray unless you note this
carefully, e.g. *eso no es el caso*, which you might be tempted to
understand as 'that's not the case' whereas it really means
'that's not the point', a rather different matter. 'That's not
the case' should be rendered *eso no es así* or even *eso no es
verdad* since 'the case' is often, in English, a sort of euphemism
for 'true'.

Ese no es el caso could also be rendered as *eso no hace al caso*
but you should distinguish *hacer al caso* carefully from *hacer
caso*, a verbal phrase which means 'to take notice', 'to pay
attention', 'to obey'. *No hizo caso*, 'He took no notice', 'He
ignored it'; *Siempre hago caso de lo que se me dice*, 'I always do
what I'm told'. The straightforward verb for 'to obey' is
obedecer but this is little used in speaking.

> *Hacer caso a . . .* (of a person)
> *Hacer caso de . . .* (of a thing)
>   (*v.* also **acaso.**)

castaña (f). Chestnut (*v.* FOOD). The word for castanets is
castañuelas as chestnut is the usual wood from which they are
made.

castizo. I include this word, not because it is important but
because it is commonly on the lips of the average *madrileño*.
It derives from *casta*, 'caste' (in the Indian sense), and means
virtually 'castey', just as 'classy' derives from 'class'. The
caste to which it refers is a certain type of 100 per cent *madrileño* and it is applied more particularly to the curious accent
which such *madrileños* use, analogous to Cockney in London.

categoría (f). It means 'category', of course, but 'category' is not
often on the lips of the average Englishman whereas *categoría*
is frequently on the lips of a Spaniard. *Es una persona de
mucha categoría*, 'He's a very important person', 'He's a big
bug', i.e. of exalted office or social status. The best concept to
connect it with is 'important', as applied to persons. It is a
strong word for 'important', *importante* being the routine word,
and in practice it is usually associated with obtaining favours,
hence, perhaps, its commonness.

cazo (m). Saucepan (with one handle) (*v.* DOM. APP.). Spanish
saucepans are not the same as ours; one of the commonest is a
deep, rotund affair with two handles, called an *olla* (*q.v.*).

cazuela (f). An earthenware dish or bowl (*v.* DOM. APP.).

cebolla (f). Onion (*v.* FOOD). It is also commonly used for the
bulb of a plant, though not of an electric bulb which is
bombilla.

cello (m). As in English, the colloquial abbreviation for *violoncello*. The *ll* is taken over from the Italian and is pronounced as though it were single, i.e. as in English (*v.* MUSIC); *violoncelo, violonchelo.*

central (f). As a noun (N.B., feminine) it means both 'telephone exchange', and 'power station'. The diminutive *centralita* is the usual word for a private telephone exchange (*v.* OFF. APP.).

cepillo (m). Brush of almost any sort (*v.* DOM. APP.).

cerdo (m). Pork, pig (*v.* FOOD). A sucking pig, however, is *cochinillo.*

cereza (f). A white or red cherry, not a cherry in general. A black cherry or a crystallised one is called a *guinda.*

cerilla (f). The usual word for a 'match' of the sort you strike.[1] The name derives from *cera*, wax, as practically all Spanish matches are of the wax variety (and very small and thin so that the technique of striking them takes a good deal of acquiring). 'Got a match?' *¿Tienes una cerilla?*

champiñón (m). Mushroom (*v.* FOOD).

charla (f), **charlar**. 'Chat', 'gas', 'jaw', though it is less slangy than the last two English equivalents given. *Estaban charlando*, 'They were chatting' (or 'chattering'), *Tener una charla*, 'To have a chat'.

chico, -a. As a noun it means 'boy' (or 'girl' as the case may be) and equates fairly closely, as it can be a boy of any age up to about 40: *Es un chico muy simpático*, 'He's a very nice boy' (e.g. as uttered by a kindly old lady). Used between men it tends to mean rather 'chap' and is employed a great deal exclamatively when it is very similar to *¡hijo!* (q.v.), though perhaps a shade less contemptuous. *¡Pero chico . . .!* 'But my good man . . .!', 'My dear chap!', i.e. mildly protesting but much commoner than either of these expressions in English.
     As an adjective it is a colloquial word for 'small' and has a slightly provincial air so that it approximates to such a word as 'wee' but is more universally used. The double diminutive *chiquitito*, 'teeny-weeny', 'minute' is also widely used.

chincheta (f). Lit. a 'little bug' (*chinche*, bug), but the normal word for 'drawing-pin' (Amer. 'thumb-tack') (*v.* OFF. APP.).

chipirones (m. pl.) A Basque word for 'squid' but frequently appears in menus (*v.* **calamares**).

[1] A 'match' of the football type is *un partido.*

chirimoya (f). Custard-apple (v. FOOD). It sounds very exotic but they grow in the South of Spain and are delicious. You cut them in half and then tackle each half with a small spoon. As with cherries, you are permitted to take the pips in your mouth and spit them out later.

chirivía (f). Parsnip (v. FOOD). Not a common vegetable in Spain.

chisme (m). A piece of gossip; frequently referred to in the plural *los chismes*, 'the gossip'; *Cuéntame los chismes*, 'Tell me all the gossip'. *Chismorreo* is another word for the same thing. *Chismorrear*, 'to gossip'. *Chisme* is also used for something you cannot remember the name of and therefore equates with 'what you may call it', 'thingummybob', etc. *¿Tienes el chisme ese?* 'Have you got that what's-its-name?'

chiste (m). A funny story, a joke. 'A low joke' is *un chiste verde* (cf. Fr. *vert* with the same meaning). 'To tell a funny story' is *contar un chiste*, and if you say 'I know a joke' (*sé un chiste*) you will probably be greeted with *¡Cuéntanos, cuéntanos!*, 'Tell us, tell us'.

chófer (m). Do not be *despistado* by the look of this word, it is merely the Spanish form of *chauffeur* and means that or 'driver' (v. CARS).

chuleta (f). Cutlet, chop (v. FOOD).

cigala (f). One of those elongated lobsters which the French call *langoustines*. They are far smaller than lobsters and I am not aware of an English word for them as they do not occur in home waters. They are sometimes sold in London as 'Dublin Bay Prawns' or 'Norway Lobsters'.

cigarro (m). A False Friend; it means a cigarette, not a cigar, which is *puro* (q.v.).

cigüeñal (m). Crankshaft (v. CARS).

cinta (f). Band, ribbon, tape. It has a multitude of different uses one of which is for a typewriter: *Cinta* (*de máquina*), 'typewriter ribbon' (v. OFF. APP.).

clarinete (m). Clarinet. A bass clarinet is *clarinete bajo* (v. MUSIC).

claro. This you will hear a hundred times a day and it means 'obviously', 'of course', 'quite so', 'naturally'. Perhaps its most frequent use is in sympathetic response to something that is being recounted to you, e.g. if someone says *No quise admitir que no tenía dinero*, 'I didn't want to admit that I hadn't any money', you would nod your head and say *¡Claro!*, 'Of course not'. By judicious use of different tones of voice you can vary it to mean anything from 'Why, you poor lamb, of course you were right!' to 'Obviously not, you great twirp!' If you want to say 'obviously' originally, as opposed to responsively, you should say *claro está*, e.g. 'Obviously I didn't want him to see me' would be *Claro está que no quise que me viese.*

Almost interchangeable with *claro* is *desde luego* (*q.v.*). (*v.* also the note under *naturalmente.*)

clave (f). Clef (*v.* MUSIC). You might have expected the usual Spanish form *llave* but this is not used in music. Beware of thinking it means 'stave' which is *pentagrama.*

clavo (m). Nail (*v.* DOM. APP.). Also, clove (*v.* FOOD).

claxon (m). Horn (*v.* CARS). *Bocina* also exists.

cliché (m). May be used for almost anything from which prints are taken but the most common meanings are 'negative', i.e. of a photograph, and stencil (*v.* OFF. APP.).

clip (m). Taken directly from the English and means a clip of the sort you clip papers together with (*v.* OFF. APP.).

cobrar (**cobrador**). To get paid for, to cash (e.g. a cheque). *Tengo que cobrar este giro* (*postal*), 'I've got to go and cash this postal order'. *Voy a cobrar*, 'I'm going to get my pay' (i.e. on pay day). *¿Cobraste?*, 'Did you get the money for it?' As you see, a curious word—for us—and one that will not come easily to your lips unless you make yourself conscious of it though it is perfectly good Spanish and not merely colloquial.

A *Cobrador* is a gentleman whom we, with our universal banking system, hardly know and would regard as wasting a shocking amount of time if we did. It is his job to go round collecting money that is owed (though not necessarily overdue). If you owe money in Spain, the normal procedure is to say, in effect, 'Come and get it', and the *Cobrador* of the firm to whom you owe it—a mere boy, as often as not, and by no means a *persona de categoría*—duly comes round and collects it from you. Every business firm, however insignificant, must have its *Cobrador*, or a *muchacho* who can act as such when necessary, and quite small businesses will often employ somebody to do nothing else. When I lived in Madrid I was a member of a club, I hired a piano, and ran up occasional bills. All the expenses would, in England, have been dealt with by cheque or banker's order but in Spain I had regular monthly visits from a nice old woman for the piano money and a nice old man for the club fee. It is typical of Spain that these old souls, in spite of the considerable sums of money that pass through their hands, receive a very tiny fraction of it for themselves, and yet are completely honest and usually charming, with no trace of self-pity. They settle down with placid, oriental patience to wait long periods for money which is owed to their employers. As indicated above, they are by no means always old; frequently they are delightful (and naughty) little boys, much too young, we should say, to be trusted with so much money, but in spite of the fact that they dawdle about their business and will almost certainly join in a brief game of football in the street on the way (with the money on their person) it is very rarely that their honesty has to be called into question. After spending some time in Spain you cease to worry about the fact that their existence involves a considerable waste of labour and come to regard the system as rather pleasant but it is really only pleasing for those who earn enough money and it would be much pleasanter if they were better paid.

Cobrador also applies to the man who collects the money in a tram or bus, and in that case, therefore, would be translated 'conductor'. *Conductor* in Spanish means driver.

cochinillo (m). A little pig (or 'little swine', as a Swedish friend once called it), i.e. a sucking pig. A common and much-prized dish in Spain (*v.* FOOD).

coger. One could write a fair-sized brochure on the uses of this verb and no doubt your grammar-book has given it some attention. If I presume to add a word it will be chiefly to give examples taken from experience.

The nearest single English word is 'get' and the two words equate in a remarkable number of contexts; not only in such simple cases as *Voy a coger un periódico*, 'I'm going to get a paper', but *Cogí frío*, 'I got cold', and *Cogió un tranvía*, 'He got a tram'. In English we are quite likely to say 'I caught cold' or 'He caught a tram', and 'catch' is certainly one of the root meanings of *coger*. *Hay que coger la pelota antes que llegue al suelo*, 'You have to catch the ball before it touches the ground' (explaining cricket to a Spaniard). As so often, too, it covers uses of the root verb plus a preposition which are so common in English without a preposition being added in Spanish, e.g. 'to get hold of': *Coge esto* means 'Get hold of this' or just *Cógelo* which could mean the same or could mean 'Catch!' or 'Here you are!' if you were to throw something across; also *Lo cogí*, 'I caught him out' (in the metaphorical sense). *¿Lo has cogido?* can often mean 'D'you understand?', i.e. 'D'you get me?'

'To get hold of' in the widest sense is probably the best concept, but be sure that it is wide. *Cógelo* would equate with 'Pick it up' if the object in question were lying on the floor, and 'Dive down and get it' if at the bottom of the swimming-pool.

col (f). Cabbage (*v.* FOOD).

colador (m). Colander.

colgar. To hang, to hang up, to hang down. Here mentioned in connection with the telephone. An operator may say, *¿Quiere colgar, por favor?*, 'Will you hang up, please?' (on many private exchanges he cannot put a call through to you unless you do); *No cuelgue*, 'Don't hang up', 'Don't ring off'.

coliflor (f). Cauliflower (v. FOOD).

collar (m). A False Friend, in its way, as it does not mean collar but necklace. Collar is *cuello*.

colocar. This is a sort of supplementary verb to *Poner*, i.e. it expresses a more precise aspect of the verb 'to put'. Quite often *poner* could be used instead but if you mean more precisely 'put away' or 'put in position' or 'put in place' then you use *colocar*. It is another case where the only difficulty is to remember to use it. If the maid says to you *La ropa está colocada* you understand easily enough that 'The linen is put away in the drawers' (or wherever its place may be) but would you have remembered, when giving her the linen, to say *Hay que colocar esta ropa en su sitio*, or would you have said *Vd. tiene que ponerla en los cajones*? Another translation could be 'set out' in the sense of 'put ready'. *Todos los naipes fueron colocados sobre la mesa*, 'The cards were all set out on the table'.

coma (m and f). When masculine it means 'coma', but feminine 'comma', and here included for the latter (v. OFF. APP.). **comillas,** inverted commas.

comida (f). Lit. meal, but in practice always the midday meal, i.e. lunch. *¿Vas a comer?* 'Will you have lunch?' The evening meal is *la cena* and 'Are you coming to dinner (supper)?' *¿Vas a venir a cenar?*

como. Means 'as', 'how', 'like', but it may also mean 'what' or 'why' in certain contexts. For example, when you have not heard properly what someone has said you can say *¿Cómo?*, i.e. 'What?' or 'What was that?' (cf. Fr. *comment?*); also *¿Cómo se llama?* 'What is it called?' or 'What's your name?' (and how well we know the foreign student who says 'How is it called?').

More idiomatic, however, is its use in cases where you pick on a word in something that has been said and question it. Most common, for picking on, is probably the word *no* and the phrase *¿Cómo que no?*, 'What d'you mean, "no"?', or 'Why not?' is a cliché and should be learnt off pat; it is not as rude as the English 'What d'you mean, no!' and in a certain tone of voice can sound very kindly: e.g. if you invite a young lady to come out and she says 'No' and you say *Pero, ¿cómo que no?* in a rather persuasive tone of voice it equates with 'Can't you really?' or 'Yes, come on'.

Como may, however, be attached to any word you please if you want to question it, e.g. someone says *¡Es una vergüenza!* and you reply, *¿Cómo vergüenza?*, i.e. 'It's disgraceful!', and the reply, 'What d'you mean, disgraceful?' or 'What's disgraceful about it?' according to your tone of voice. Sometimes a more likely English equivalent would be not a question but a statement which accepts the query and goes beyond it, i.e. 'Yes, but there's not really any disgrace about it', or 'Do you really think it is disgraceful?'[1] The English are on the whole sophisticated in comparison with the Spanish, who accept simplicity as a convention though it by no means follows that they are simple.[2]

comodín (m). Joker (v. CARDS).

compás (m). Normally it means compass, of the sort you draw circles with (or the direction-finder —also *brújula*) but it is here included as it means a bar in music (i.e. the interval, not the line which is *barra*, q.v.). A conductor rehearsing an orchestra may say 'Start two bars before figure 27' and in Spanish this would be *Empiecen dos compases antes del 27*; 'You're a bar ahead (behind)', *Va adelantado (retrasado) un compás*; 'There are four beats to the bar', *Hay cuatro tiempos por compás*[3] (though if it is a matter of the conductor beating four to a bar, e.g. 'I'm taking this in four' the expression is *Esto es a cuatro*. A well-thumbed orchestral score in Spain is likely to have '*a 2*', '*a 4*', etc., scrawled in pencil at the beginning of any given section.)

A 1st time bar is called *Compás de primera*, and a 2nd, *de segunda*. A bar for nothing is *Un compás libre* (v. MUSIC).

completo. By itself it means 'full up', and you will see it in the front of trams and buses. I am more concerned, however, to draw your attention to the expression *Por completo* which is probably the best translation of our colloquial 'absolutely'. You may say *completamente*, but *por completo* is rather stronger as well as being more colloquial: *Se arruinó por completo*, 'He was absolutely ruined'.

compras (f). Lit. purchases, but used where we should talk of shopping: *Tengo que hacer unas compras*, 'I've got some shopping to do' (cf., Fr. *achats*). A current expression for 'to go shopping' is *ir de compras*; *Fué de compras*, 'He (she) went shopping'.

concretar. In English we have the adjective 'concrete' (i.e. in the metaphorical sense) but we do not extend to the verb. If we did we should find it very useful and *concretar* is very useful in Spanish though it is not especially colloquial. *Yo quería concretar este asunto*, 'I wanted to get this matter fixed up'. It can also be translated 'to summarise', e.g. a professor at the end of a lecture: 'Let us summarise the main points', *Vamos a concretar los puntos principales*.

[1] I cannot help feeling that if, as suggested under **caber**, the Mad Hatter's Tea Party had called out *¡No cabe! ¡No cabe!* Alice would instinctively have replied *¿Cómo que no quepo?* whereas in fact she replied 'There's plenty of room'.
[2] Once again this is a generalisation; what could be more modern and sophisticated than *enchufado* (q.v.)?
[3] There is a word for a 'four-beat-bar', viz. *cuaternario*, but it is not of vital importance.

condensador (m). Condenser (*v.* CARS).

conducir, conductor. *Conducir* is an Unreliable Friend: it may mean 'to conduct' but is far more often likely to mean 'to drive' (a car), *¿Quién va a conducir?* 'Who's going to drive?' And it certainly does not mean 'to conduct' in the musical sense which is *dirigir*.

Conductor, the noun, is equally unreliable. Applied to a person it means 'driver'. A musical conductor is a *director* or a *maestro*; a bus conductor is a *cobrador* (*q.v.*). *Conductor* and *conducir* only become good friends when applied to things, e.g. electricity.

conferencia (f). Amigo Informal. It means (*a*) lecture, i.e. of the sort given in lecture-halls and (*b*) long-distance telephone call, trunk call. It does also mean 'conference' and 'interview'.

confianza, de. An adjectival phrase meaning 'trustworthy' as well as 'in confidence': *Todo esto es de confianza*, 'All this is in confidence' (but *Le digo esto en confianza*, 'I'm telling you this in confidence). It frequently comes up in connection with domestics where we should use the word 'honest': *Es una chica de confianza*, 'She's an honest girl (maid)', but it can be used of anyone who can be trusted in particular circumstances: *El es de confianza*, 'He's all right', 'You can trust him'.

conforme. In agreement, I agree; interrogatively 'Do you agree?' The whole expression is *estar conforme*, 'to be in agreement', and 'I agree', should really be *Estoy conforme*; 'Do you agree?', *¿Está conforme?*, etc.

For other words for 'agree' *v.* **acuerdo, convenir.**

conseguir. 'To get', in the sense of 'to obtain' but used when the getting implies a certain amount of difficulty, so that 'to get hold of' or 'to obtain' is nearer the mark: *Tendremos que conseguir entradas para los toros* (*o billetes para el tren*), 'We shall have to get hold of tickets for the bull-fight' (or 'railway tickets') and anyone who knew Spain a few years ago will be aware that it was not always an easy matter and that the black market had frequently to be resorted to, even for the latter.[1]

When *conseguir* is used with a verb instead of a noun it has the force of 'to succeed in', 'to contrive to', 'to manage to': *¿Has conseguido entrar?*, 'Did you succeed in getting in?', 'Did you manage to get in?'

'Obtain' is perhaps the best word to bear in mind.

conservas (f). Preserves, but it has no suggestion, for the Spanish mind, of fruit or jam. It suggests rather tins of meat or fish but it is a comprehensive word for any preserved food whatever (*v.* FOOD).

[1] Another word for 'to get' is *recoger* (*q.v.*), but the difference may be illustrated by the example given above; if you said *Tenemos que recoger las entradas* it would suggest that they had already been ordered and that you had only to pick them up.

constipado. A classic Falso Amigo; it means 'having a cold': *Estoy (un poco) constipado*, 'I've got (a bit of) a cold'. Many a poor Spaniard, and perhaps even the nation's conventions, must have been misjudged through ignorance of this. The Spanish for 'constipated' is *estreñido*.

contabilidad (f). Accounts in general.

contable (m. or f., according to sex). Accountant (*v.* OFF. APP.).

contador (m). Lit. a counter, i.e. a machine that counts and therefore 'meter' (*v.* DOM. APP.).

contrabajo (m). Double-bass (*v.* MUSIC).

contrafagot (m). Contrabassoon, double bassoon (*v.* MUSIC).

contralto (f). I call it feminine as it normally applies to the contralto of a choir who, in modern times, is usually female. Formerly it was a male voice, hence, no doubt, the masculine ending and if you are concerned with boys' choirs then it will be masculine, but if with mixed choirs then you say *las contraltos*.

N.B. The abbreviation 'altos' which we use in English cannot be applied in Spain, as the word *alto* means high. In my early days in Spain, when interviewing ladies with a view to singing in a choir, I sometimes said *¿Puede cantar alto?* and was disconcerted when they replied *No muy alto*.

convenir. Most often used in the 3rd person: *conviene, convenía, convino*, etc., and, of course, means 'to be convenient' in its basic concept though it can emerge in a surprisingly diverse number of English equivalents. For *No me conviene* we should quite often say, 'It's not what I want' or 'I don't like it', e.g. when choosing some article in a shop. *¿Le conviene?* would be 'Is that all right?', 'Does that suit you?', e.g. when fixing a dentist's appointment. If a bag will not fit into the back of a car *No conviene* means 'It's the wrong shape', 'It won't fit' (whereas *no cabe* (*q.v.*) means 'there's no room for it').

Obviously the translation would often be 'to be convenient', much less often 'to agree' (as in French). For words for 'agree', *v.* **acuerdo, conforme.**

convertirse. A perfectly good expression for 'to turn into', e.g. *La bruja se convirtió en una rana*, 'The witch turned into a frog'; it is not colloquial but I mention it as it is another possible translation for 'to become' (*v.* also **hacerse, pasar, volverse**).

copas (f). Approximately 'hearts', but it applies only to Spanish playing-cards; the usual word is *corazones* (*q.v.*).

copia (f). The straightforward word for 'copy', but used by itself where we might say 'carbon copy' (*v.* OFF. APP.).

corazón (m). Heart, of course, but also Hearts (*v.* CARDS).

corbata (f). The Spanish form of the word 'cravat' and the usual word for a 'tie' of the type men wear.

corchea (f). A quaver (v. MUSIC).

cordero (m). Mutton (or sheep) (v. FOOD). It has nothing to do with cobblers, as those who know French may tend to imagine. A cobbler is *un zapatero*.

corno inglés (m). Cor anglais, English horn (v. MUSIC). It is taken from the Italian, hence the 'corno'; the Spanish version of this Latin word is *cuerno* which is the proper word when applied to a bull, etc., or even to a 'hunting-horn' which is *cuerno de caza*.

correa (del ventilador) (f). Fan-belt (v. CARS).

corriente. Ordinary, usual, routine. A perusal of Falsos Amigos (p. 118) will make you aware that the Spanish for 'ordinary' is not *ordinario*; in most cases it is *corriente* or *regular*. The Spanish for *vin ordinaire* is *vino corriente*. *Corriente* is both the noun and the adjective for current, even for electric current, though on the frequent occasions when the electric current is cut off it is more usual to hear *No hay luz* than *No hay corriente*. As a noun it is feminine.

cortar (v.t.). To cut, including for cards (q.v.), also 'cut off', 'cut away', 'cut out'. It is the usual expression for 'to cut off' on the telephone: *No me corte*, 'Don't cut me off'; *No corte*, 'Don't ring off' (although *No cuelgue*, 'Don't hang up'); *Han cortado la luz*, 'The electric current's gone off'.

qué cosa más —! 'What a — thing!' or 'How —!' or 'Isn't it —!' *¡Qué cosa más rara!* or *¡Qué cosa tan rara!* 'How funny', 'How extraordinary!' *¡Qué película más aburrida!*, 'Can you imagine a more boring film!' After a long and acrimonious argument with her son at a meal-table, a Spanish woman I know exclaimed to the table at large: *¡Qué hijo más antipático!* It is hard to imagine an adequate English translation: 'There's a nice son for you!' is probably nearest the mark and reflects a certain difference in the national temperaments. As you see, the word *más* is applied in this sense to all manner of words besides *cosa*.

Italian scholars should note that such Italian expressions as '*Cosa dice?*' ('What do you say?') are *not* used in Spanish; you would say *¿Qué dice?* though it is a little abrupt and *perdone* is more polite.

croissant (pronounced cruasán).

cruceta (f). Universal joint (v. CARS).

cuanto antes. As soon as possible, right away: *Hay que hacerlo cuanto antes*, 'It's got to be done right away'; *Cuanto antes mejor*, 'The sooner the better'.

cuaternario (m). A four-beat-bar (*v.* MUSIC). It is not much used.

cubierta (f). Tire, i.e. the outer case (*v.* CARS).

cubo (m). Bucket or garbage can (*v.* DOM. APP.).

cuello (m). Both a neck and a collar (*v.* DOM. APP.).

cuenta (f). Lit. account, but *darse cuenta*, which is tremendously common, is the normal way of conveying 'to realise'. *No me di cuenta de eso*, 'I didn't realise that' (rather more slangy would be *No caí en eso*, 'I didn't tumble to that') (*v.* **caigo**). *Hay que darse cuenta de que*, 'You mustn't forget that . . . , must realise that . . .'.
Another common use of the word is with *tener*. *No tiene cuenta* means 'There's no point in (it)'. *¿Tiene cuenta salir esta noche?*, 'Is there any point in going out this evening?', 'Is it worth going out this evening?'
Tener en cuenta, 'to take into account'.
Cuenta, 'bill' in a restaurant (*v.* FOOD).

cuentakilómetros (m). Odometer (*v.* CARS). For speedometer (*v. indicador*). *Cuentakilómetros* is often loosely used for the latter, just as we often use 'speedometer' for the former.

cuerda (f). Cord, string, rope. Included here as it is the word for 'strings' in an orchestra. N.B. It is usually singular: 'Concerto for piano and strings', *Concierto para piano y cuerda*; 'The strings', *La cuerda*, though *Las cuerdas* may be used.

¡cuidado! (interj.) The normal word for 'Look out!', 'Take care!' (Fr. *Attention!*, German, *Achtung!*). *Hay que tener cuidado*, 'You have to be careful' ('*Il faut faire attention*') (*v.* MUSIC).

culpa (f). Blame, fault. Bear it in mind and warn yourself off *falta* which is something of a Falso Amigo (*falta*, 'default'). *La culpa es mía*, 'It's my fault'; *¿De quién es la culpa?*, 'Whose fault is it?' *Echar la culpa*, 'to push the blame on to somebody else' (*v.* **echar**).

cursi. Means *chi-chi*, if you know French; in English, 'affected', 'namby-pamby', 'spivvish', 'lah-di-dah', *nouveau-riche*, 'posh', 'pretentious', 'snobbish'—a sort of compound of all these. A new, smart, self-conscious and expensive restaurant which, for a while, all the rich, smart, self-conscious and expensive people regard as fashionable, would probably be called *cursi*. It is not an important word and I mention it simply because you are likely to hear it, not because I think you should use it; it may be dead in thirty years' time—or less in these days of social revolution.

D

dar. To deal (at cards, *v.* CARDS).

Dar is used a great deal in contexts where the concept is 'yield' (e.g. of results) or 'produce'. A very common expression which should be memorised is *¿Qué más da?* (lit. 'What more does it yield?') which, via 'What difference does it make?', has come to mean 'Never mind!' It could be translated 'What's the odds?' but the Spanish expression is friendly, whereas the English is sometimes a little sarcastic. 'Don't mention it!' would equate in many contexts, but is perhaps a shade formal; 'It's quite all right' perhaps is better.

A similar use of the verb is *(me) da lo mismo*, '(I) don't mind', 'It's all the same (to me)'. A common alternative for this is *Es igual.* Further examples of the use of *dar* are: *¿No te da vergüenza?*, 'Doesn't it make you ashamed?'; *El reloj acaba de dar las cinco*, 'The clock has just struck five'; *dar la vuelta*, 'to turn round' (i.e. to do a right about turn); *dar gusto*, 'to give pleasure'; *dar la lata* (slightly slangy but extremely common), 'to make a nuisance of one's self' (*v.* **lata**). *Dar aire*, 'to pump' (air into tires)'.

decepción, -ado. A Falso Amigo: *Decepción*, 'disappointment' and *decepcionado*, 'disappointed'. 'Deception', *engaño*; and 'deceived', *engañado*.

delco (m). Distributor (*v.* CARS).

depósito (m). Deposit, but also petrol-tank (*v.* CARS).

descanso (m). Rest, relief, relaxation, off-season, interval, break. You will probably see it most often on the wind-screens of taxis. If the notice is *Libre* the taxi may be hailed; if there is no notice, the driver already has a fare; if the notice is *Descanso* he has no fare but will ignore your hailing as it is his lunch-time, or at any rate he feels like a rest. Very occasionally he may be prevailed upon to change his mind when a large tip is obviously indicated and the promise of it may be needed to induce him to do so. Shops occasionally put up a *Descanso* notice when they close for the lunch-hour but the proper word for this is *Cerrado*. *Descanso* is more appropriate for individuals, and equates with 'Back in ten minutes' (or whatever period it may be; Spaniards, very wisely, do not specify). It is, however, the proper word for an 'interval' in the theatre or for a mid-morning 'break'.

The verb *descansar* is as common as the noun. *Voy a descansar un rato* is 'I'm going to have a little rest', though if it is forty winks after lunch the word *siesta* may well be employed, e.g. *Voy a echarme una siestecita* (*v.* DIMINUTIVES).

desde luego. Of course, naturally, quite so. I have never succeeded in satisfying myself as to why this expression means what it does but this is all the more reason for learning it off pat.[1] *Claro* (*q.v.*) may also be used in most contexts but as it can sometimes sound rather sarcastic I recommend *desde luego*. You will need it twenty times a day. I am unable to think up a colloquial context where it would not be a satisfactory translation of 'of course' so I shall not bother you with examples.

desgracia, -damente. A Falso Amigo as it does not mean 'disgrace' but 'misfortune'. *Desgraciadamente* is the proper translation of 'unfortunately' (though for 'fortunately' you must say *afortunadamente* as *graciadamente* is not permissible). *¡Qué desgracia!*, 'What a misfortune!'; 'How unfortunate!', 'What bad luck!' 'Disgrace' is **vergüenza** (*q.v.*).

desmayarse, desmayo (m). A Falso Amigo: it does not mean 'dismay', it means 'faint', 'swoon'; and the verb is reflexive in this sense; *ella se desmayó*, 'she fainted'. 'Dismay' is *descorazonamiento*.

despacho (m). An 'office', yes, but of an individual person, e.g. 'I've left it in my office', *Lo he dejado en mi despacho*. The 'office' in general is *la oficina*, e.g. *Voy a la oficina*, 'I'm going to the office' (*v.* OFF. APP.).

despacio. Slow.

despistar, despiste (m). A very common verb meaning 'to push off the track', 'to mislead' in both the literal and metaphorical senses. *Me había despistado*, 'I had lost my way'; *Eso me despistó por completo*, 'That put me completely off the rails (or scent)'. The adjective is *despistado*, 'bewildered', 'absentminded': *Estoy despistado*, 'I'm all at sea'; *un hombre despistado*, 'an absent-minded fellow'.

The noun *despiste* can refer to 'going off the rails' in most senses; in particular connection with the cars it is most likely to mean a skid (*v.* CARS) (though *patinazo* is more precise for this). *Tiene un despiste inmenso*, 'He doesn't know what to do next'.

destornillador (m). Screwdriver. Strictly speaking it means an unscrew-driver, but this, after all, is an equally important half of its functions (*v.* DOM. APP. and CARS).

diamantes (m. pl.). Diamonds in all senses, including cards (*q.v.*).

dictar. To dictate (*v.* OFF. APP.).

diferencial (f). Differential (*v.* CARS).

dificultar. 'To make difficult', 'to raise difficulties', but not necessarily 'to obstruct' in any intentional sense which is

---

[1] *Naturalmente* is not incorrect but *desde luego* is a great deal more common and if you want to sound authentic I suggest you implant it in its place. *Naturalmente* would be used in writing (e.g. business letters).

better rendered by *estorbar*. I mention it chiefly as it is often used where we should say 'interfere', e.g. 'His father's death interfered with his studies', *La muerte de su padre dificultó sus estudios*. You might say '. . . *interrumpió sus estudios*' but this suggests that it stopped them altogether whereas *dificultó* suggests that it upset them temporarily. 'Interfere' is not a very easy word to translate. *Interferir* exists but is confined to technical and scientific contexts. In other contexts you have to consider the exact meaning and decide what form of interference is intended. *Dificultar* and *estorbar* indicate two forms. For another, see **meterse**.

diga, digo. Obviously ordinary parts of the verb *decir* but some of their uses deserve attention. *Diga* or *Dígame* (*dime* for intimate friends) is extremely common on the telephone (*q.v.*, p. 143) and means virtually 'Hallo!' although literally it is 'Speak to me!' Certainly 'speak to me' or 'say on' has to be the basic concept but you must cast your net wide. Suppose you get into a taxi and are too preoccupied to have told the driver where to go, he may say, to remind you, *Dígame, señor* (or *Vd. dirá*), 'Where to, sir?' A waiter may come up to your table to receive your order, or a shop assistant to ask you what you want, and say the same. The English would be simply 'Yes?' or 'Yes, sir?' in an interrogative tone of voice.

Digo is the word for 'I mean' when you have made a mistake in speaking and are correcting yourself, e.g. *El se lo dió—digo ella se lo dió*, 'He gave it to him—I mean *she* gave it to him'. You could say *Quiero decir* or, better, *Mejor dicho*, but *digo* is the most common. Where 'I mean' is not to correct a mistake but to introduce an explanation, *v.* **o sea.**

Digo yo is a cliché for 'so *I* think', 'at any rate that's *my* opinion', 'them's my sentiments', and the *yo* consequently gets a certain emphasis.

No me digas is another cliché meaning 'Go on!' 'You don't say', 'Never!' It is usually said a little sarcastically and is rather familiar, hence the second person singular.

Dios. Yes, the Almighty, but to our Northern ideas it is remarkable how readily, in an extremely religious country, His name is taken in vain. All members of the Holy Family have furnished Christian names to Catholic Spain—*José, María, Jesús, Concepción, Asunción* (a woman's name), etc.[1] I have come across some very naughty little boys named *Jesús* and a perusal of police court news in the papers indicates that there are naughty big boys too: indeed I read of one who was executed. If, however, the Spaniards decline to go as far as *Dios* for a Christian name they have no compunction in scattering God's name about their conversation. *Por Dios* is literally 'For

[1] Famous virgins also supply names; there is a *Virgen del Prado* with the result that *Prado* is a girl's name.

God's sake!' or 'Good God!' but it is nothing like so strong as in English, in fact it frequently means merely 'Please, do', and is then excessively polite. *¡Siéntese, por Dios!* means 'Do please sit down', and if someone says, 'Do you mind if I smoke?' you hasten to assure them *¡Pero, por Dios!* (in French *'Mais je vous en prie'*) and in English probably 'I'm so sorry!' (i.e. for not having suggested it earlier). In practice you would probably also add the words *No faltaba más* (v. **falta**).

Another common and fairly mild expression is *Dios mío* for which an equation would perhaps be, 'Oh, Lor'!' or 'Good Heavens!' or perhaps 'Damn!' It is not quite the same as the French *'Mon Dieu!'* which, as often as not, is merely a substitute for a nervous little laugh or a moment of mild exasperation or a brief pause for consideration. In Spanish, worry is indicated and sometimes even distress. If a woman laddered her stocking she would probably exclaim *¡Ay, Dios mío!*, and if she said it in a piercing shriek this would serve to receive the news that her child had been run over, but muttered quietly by a typist it could simply mean that she had put the carbons in the wrong way round.

The main thing to appreciate is that the word as such does not startle Spanish ears. It is true that the worst possible expressions in Spain are blasphemous ones but these are concocted by associating the divine with certain functions all too human and it is the contrast which shocks; in any case the holy of holies, for a Spaniard, is not God, nor even His Son, but the Sacrament.[1]

The Son figures in a rather odd place where you might not expect Him, namely when anyone sneezes. The Spanish for 'Bless you!' is *¡Jesús!* and the automatic response is *gracias*. 'Bless you!' has gone out in England and perhaps *Jesús* is on its way out in Spain but it remains to a considerable extent.

Another common ejaculation, perhaps slightly stronger than *¡Dios mío!* is *¡Madre mía!*

dirección (f). An Amigo Informal. It does mean 'direction' but it also means 'address': *Le daré su dirección*, 'I'll give you his address'. Perhaps more common, however, is *señas*: *¿Puede darme sus señas?* 'Can you give me his (her, your) address?' It should be noted that Spaniards *do* say, e.g. *Dirección única* for 'One-way traffic' and not *sentido único* on the lines of the French *'sens unique'*.

In a car *dirección* means 'the steering' (v. CARS).

disco (m). The dial of a telephone, as well as many other types of disc, e.g. a gramophone record. For the verb 'to dial', *v.* **marcar**.

disgustado. Hardly a Buen Amigo as it means, as near as may be, 'displeased': *Estoy muy disgustado con ese gramófono*, 'I'm

---

[1] And consequently one of the most soul-blenching of Spanish oaths associates the sacramental with the scatological.

awfully fed up about that gramophone'; *Estoy disgustado con ella*, 'I'm disappointed in her'; *Estoy disgustado contigo*, 'I'm displeased with you'. It is almost invariably used with *estar* (the last example could not be rendered as *me disgustas*).

disonancia (f). Discord (*v.* MUSIC).

distinto. A Falso Amigo. It does not mean 'distinct', it means 'different', and is the usual word for this, though *diferente* can be used. 'Distinct' would be *visible* or *claro*.

divertido. Like *aburrido* ('bored' or 'boring') this means 'amused' or 'amusing'. 'And then a most amusing thing happened', *Y luego pasó la cosa más divertida.* Q. 'How did you like the show?' A. 'Most amusing!' Q. *¿Qué tal el teatro?* A. *Muy divertido.* Illogical, but there it is! And it is no use inventing *divertiente* and trying to make it work; I've tried it and they will not accept it. *Divertido* it is.

do. C in MUSIC (*q.v.*). It does not mean 'doh' which has to be referred to as *la tónica* (*q.v.*).

dominante (f). Dominant (*v.* MUSIC).

dos puntos. Colon (in punctuation) (*v.* OFF. APP.).

¿duele? 'Does it hurt?' Usually with the personal pronoun. Q. *¿Le duele?*, 'Does it hurt?' A. *Sí, me duele,* 'Yes, it does'. No doubt you know this when you carefully think out the conjugation of *doler* but as the 3rd person singular present indicative is by far the commonest form you may as well learn it off pat (along with *me dolía* and *me dolió* in the background just in case).

dueño, -a. The chief personage in a given connection; it normally implies the owner, e.g. of a shop or a business: 'the lady of the house', *la dueña de la casa*.[1] I mention it here as it is the usual word for landlord or landlady.

E

echar. This is a tremendously common verb with a multitude of different meanings, some of them extremely colloquial and even slangy; it is another of the words on which a whole brochure could be written and even then you could not always be sure of using it correctly. To master it a good many years' residence in Spain would be necessary.

The etymology of the word is revealing: it is a corruption of the Latin '*ejectare*' and the basic concept is 'to out' in the widest sense of the word, e.g. 'to throw out', 'push out', 'pour out', 'emit', 'shake out', 'gush out', etc. *¿Lo echo?* would

---

[1] Our word 'duenna' derives from it.

mean 'Shall I pour it out?' if the tea had just been brought in, but *¿Le echo?* would be 'Shall I chuck him out?' if referring to some undesirable person. Basically it is a perfectly proper word and would be the normal literary word for 'throw', 'eject', 'emit', etc., but it is used in practice in innumerable contexts where an Englishman might, in an undiscriminating mood, say 'chuck', 'shove', 'heave', 'smack', and the like. You can perhaps get a bird's-eye view if I quote some examples:

Me echó la culpa, 'He pushed the blame on to me'.

Echa el freno, 'Put the brake on' (as it were 'Stick the old brake on').

Vamos a echar un vistazo a, 'Let's go and have a look at' (i.e. 'throw a glance at').

Echar la llave, 'To lock up' (i.e. 'give the key a push round').

Vamos a echar tierra sobre el asunto, 'Let's forget it' (i.e. 'chuck earth on it').

Echar chispas, 'To be very angry' (i.e. 'to emit sparks').

¿Qué echan?, 'What's on?' (cinema, radio, etc.) (i.e. 'What are they emitting?').

A curious idiomatic phrase is *echar de menos* which means 'to miss' in the sense of 'to feel the want of': *Le echo de menos*, 'I miss him'; *Se le echaba mucho de menos*, 'He was sorely missed'. If, however, you decided to translate *The Mikado* into Spanish—a proceeding I do not in the least recommend —you could have a good deal of trouble with 'They'd none of them be missed' since *A ninguno de ellos se le echaría de menos* simply sounds ridiculous; the straightforward, unridiculous translation is *No se notaría la falta de ninguno* and gone is Gilbert's pungency.

eje (m). Axle (*v.* CARS). Also 'axis'; *El Eje* (*Roma/Berlín*) was a common phrase some few years ago.

embarazada. Another classic Falso Amigo and of special danger to ladies. Do not, ladies, say, as I have heard several of your sisters say, *Estoy muy embarazada* when you mean 'I am very embarrassed', 'I feel so ashamed'; say *Estoy muy confusa*. *Embarazada* means 'pregnant', 'in the family way', hence my putting it in the feminine form. Strictly speaking it means 'heavily burdened' but this is by now archaic.

'Embarrassing' may be translated *violento*. 'It was an embarrassing moment', *Fué un momento muy violento* (*q.v.*).

embrague (m). Clutch (*v.* CARS).

emoción (f). A very Unreliable Friend. The meaning it immediately suggests to a Spaniard is excitement, and *emocionar* is the normal verb for 'to excite'. *Se emocionó* does not mean 'he burst into tears' but 'he got excited' and *un estado emocionado* means 'an excited state' not 'an emotional state'.

If you wanted to say 'He could not hide his emotion' you would probably say *No pudo ocultar sus sentimientos* and 'an emotional state' would best be rendered by *un estado sentimental*. Where, however, 'emotion' is used in English in the general sense and not in particular connection with tears then *emoción* is a correct translation.

empalme (m). Junction or fork, applied either to roads or railways. There is nothing particularly colloquial about it but as you are likely to use one of the two methods of transport it is as well to be conscious of it. It can also mean 'connection' or 'branch' in engineering.

empezar. To begin; mentioned here for the benefit of musicians: 'Begin two bars before figure 27', *Empiecen dos compases antes del 27*.

encabezamiento (m). Heading, e.g. of notepaper, of a paragraph (*v.* OFF. APP.).

encantado, -a. This is the usual thing to say when you are introduced to anybody (another is *mucho gusto*) and therefore means 'How d'you do?' or, in American 'Pleased to meet you' (Fr. *enchanté*). Literally, of course, it means 'delighted' and is frequently used apart from introductions, to mean this or 'Only too pleased', 'But of course! Do come!' etc. I mention the feminine form as ladies have the complication of remembering to refer to themselves as feminine and say *encantada*.

The verb *encantar* is a common one. *Me encanta* means 'I love it', and the adjective *encantador* (*-a*) is the usual word for 'charming', 'simply lovely'. It is a strong adjective. To refer to a young woman as *encantadora* is to give high praise and it can take a strong accent. You would not, therefore, say *muy encantadora* for 'very charming'.

encender. To light, to switch on: *¿Le importaría encender la luz?* 'Would you mind switching the light on?'; *Estaba encendiendo un pitillo*, 'He was lighting a cigarette' (*v.* DOM. APP.). *Encendido* (m) is the word for 'ignition' (*v.* CARS).

enchufar. To plug in (an electrical appliance) (*v.* DOM. APP.). It gives rise to a common adjective, viz.: **enchufado**. This means literally 'plugged in' (*un enchufe*, 'an electric plug'), but metaphorically it means 'having the right contacts', i.e. on the 'Old Boy' network. A young friend of mine who was obliged to do his *Mili* (i.e. Military Service) frequently referred to other young soldiers who never went near the barracks as *bien enchufados*; their 'Old Boy' contacts—or more often their fathers'—made such duties unnecessary. It is, perhaps, characteristic of Spain that he bore them no malice therefor; he would have done the same if he could.

un enchufe is the noun for a 'contact' in this sense but it has come to mean 'a good job' or even 'a sinecure', i.e. the kind of job you can only get through being *bien enchufado*; basically, of course, it is an 'electric plug' (*v.* DOM. APP.).

encima. This is not especially colloquial but English-speakers have a tendency to say *arriba* by mistake. 'On top' is usually the best translation, whereas *arriba* is normally best translated 'above' or 'up'. *Se puso la maleta en el suelo y luego la máquina de escribir encima*, 'The portmanteau was put on the floor and then the typewriter on top of it'. 'Stick it on top', *Ponlo (póngalo) encima*. It does in fact mean literally 'on top' since *cima* is a normal word for the 'summit' of a mountain.

encontrar. You no doubt think of this as meaning 'meet', but in practice it frequently does not and almost classifies as a Falso Amigo; most often the equivalent is 'find'. *No lo encuentro* is 'I can't find it' and the verb *hallar* is far less often used. If you are going to meet somebody at the station or airport you usually say *Voy a esperarle* not *encontrarle*. If, however, you meet somebody by chance in the street (or else-where) then you should say *Le encontré por casualidad por la calle (o en otro sitio)*. The best concept is certainly 'to find'. *Hay que seguir hasta que se encuentre*, 'You have to go on until you find it'.

engranado. Geared (*v.* CARS). *Engranajes* means 'gears' but more strictly in the sense of 'gear-teeth'. What we roughly refer to as 'the gears' are in Spanish roughly referred to as *los cambios* ('the changes') or *las velocidades* ('the speeds').

enhorabuena (f). Congratulations! 'To congratulate' is *Dar la enhorabuena*. *Tengo que darle la enhorabuena*, 'I must con-gratulate you'.

ensalada, -illa (f). Both forms mean salad but *ensalada* refers to the lettuce type of thing, with or without tomatoes, beetroot, etc., whereas *ensaladilla* means 'vegetable' or 'Russian' salad, i.e. diced vegetables in mayonnaise.

enseñar. The usual word for 'to show'; *mostrar* means 'to exhibit' but is never used colloquially. French may lead one astray here since *montrer* is 'to show' and *enseigner* 'to teach'. *¿Quieres enseñarme tus fotografías?*, 'Will you show me your photographs?'

entender. A Falso Amigo for those who know French as it does not mean 'to hear' but 'to understand'; 'to hear' is nearly always dealt with by *oír*. French is apt to lead one astray in this case. The old French *ouir* does survive in such odd words as *oui* and *oyez, oyez, oyez*, but otherwise it has been almost entirely replaced by *entendre*, whereas in Spanish *oír* survives in full, and *entender* is, therefore, available for other things. Even in French, however, they say '*bien entendu*', meaning 'well understood', 'of course', and this is just the meaning of *entender*. A Spaniard, knowing you are a foreigner, is likely to interrupt himself occasionally to say *¿Entiende Vd.?*, 'Do you understand?'; 'Do you follow me?', and if you are not following you say *No entiendo* (*Je ne comprends pas*). There is sometimes discussion as to the difference between *entender* and *comprender* and it must be admitted that in practice there is often very little, but in so far as there is, it is that *entender* is to understand a person's words whereas *comprender* means to seize their total significance. *Le entiendo pero no le comprendo* would be an intelligible sentence in Spanish.[1]

enterarse. To inform oneself, to find out. *Voy a enterarme*, 'I'm going to find out'. *Está muy bien enterado*, 'He is very well informed'. *Me he enterado que el tren sale a las tres*, 'I've discovered that the train leaves at three o'clock'. Quite straightforward but if you are not conscious of the word it always suggests other things. It is not necessarily colloquial but freely used in speech.

entremeses (m. pl.). Hors d'œuvres (*v.* FOOD). They are usually excellent in Spain which is not altogether surprising as so many of the constituents are native products: sardines, anchovies, olives, tomatoes, etc. You will not, however, normally find eggs included as it is the Spanish practice to have eggs, cooked in one form or another, as a separate course (*v.* **huevos**).

envío (m). Despatch, sending off (*v.* OFF. APP.).

escabeche (m). Tinned *bonito* (*q.v.*), and other fish .

escala (f). A scale in music. Normally it means a rope-ladder (a wooden one, or a staircase, would be *escalera*). Cf. Rossini's '*La scala di seta*' which in Spanish is *La escala de seda*. It may not have been strictly 'rope' but at any rate it was *cuerda* (*q.v.*).

escape (m). Exhaust (*v.* CARS).

escoba (f). A long-handled broom (*v.* DOM. APP.). *Escobilla* (f) is used for the brushes of a dynamo or electric motor (*v.* CARS).

escribir. There is no separate Spanish word for 'to type'; they use the expression *escribir a máquina* but in ordinary office circumstances the *a máquina* is understood so that *escribir* means not only 'to write' but 'to type'. Another way of putting it is *Pasar a máquina: ¿Quieres pasar esta carta a máquina?* 'Will you type this letter?' If you want to emphasise the handwriting aspect you have to add *a mano* (*v.* OFF. APP.).

eso, esto (-e, -a). We usually pick up from our grammar-books that *este* means 'this' and *ese* means 'that', but in practice it is

[1] There is, of course, a meaning of *comprender* which *entender* would certainly not cover, viz. 'to comprehend', 'to embrace', 'to include', cf. the opening lines of Gibbon's *Decline and Fall*, 'The Empire of Rome comprehended the fairest part of the earth'.

nothing like so simple.[1] These two meanings would only apply so directly if the two are contrasted and even then not automatically. A contrasted 'that' is very often *aquel* (*-llo, -lla*). Conversely a contrasted *este* or *ese* may not be translated 'this' and 'that'. In business letters it is usual to distinguish between the two ends, i.e. the writer and the addressee, by using *este* and *ese*; e.g. you work for an organisation and are writing to a society and you say *Este organismo ha enviado a esa Sociedad*, which in English would simply be 'We sent you' or 'We sent your society'—the general distinction being 'we' and 'you' or 'our' and 'your'.

When there is no contrast the most commonly used word is probably *esto*. *¿Qué es esto?* is more often likely to be 'What's that?' than 'What's this?' though it can mean either. *En este caso* is 'in that case' and it is comparatively rare for us to say 'in this case'. When the meaning is 'that over there', e.g. 'that man over there', the translation is not *ese* but *aquel*. *Aquel hombre*, 'That man'. There are also a remarkable number of cases where 'that' is inescapable in English but it is not used at all in Spanish, e.g. 'As high as that' (indicating by a gesture how high) would be *Así de alto*; 'Yes, but not as long (or whatever it may be) as all that', *Sí, pero no tanto* simply. I tried to get Señor de Heras to translate the following anecdote from Elsie and Doris Waters: 'I was in the butcher's the other day, 'aving a chat, an' old Mother Riley come in; she pushed past me an' she says, "Gimme twopen-worth o' cat's meat, quick!", then she turned round to me an' she says, "You don't mind, do you?" an' I says, "No, not if you're as 'ungry as all *that*!"' He appreciated the story but confessed that for effective purposes it was not translatable, i.e. that although it is technically possible to translate the last sentence, the result would not raise a laugh because there would not be such sarcastic emphasis on the final 'that'.[2]

Ese is very frequently inverted in its position; in colloquial Spanish it is almost as common to hear *el señor ese* for 'that man' as *ese señor*; 'Well, when is this blessed train coming?' would be *¿Pues cuándo va a llegar el tren ese?* This, however, implies a derogatory concept.

There are also one or two clichés which are worth learning, e.g. *¡Eso es!* 'That's it' or 'That's right'. You guess and guess and at last you get it right and then they tell you *Eso es* with a very long first 'e'. Another is *Por eso*, 'For that reason', 'That's why'. 'There was a *fiesta* on Wednesday and yet you

---

[1] Classical scholars may derive some benefit and interest from considering the Latin origins:

Este, esta, esto are derived from			*Iste, ista, istud.*
Ese, esa, eso	,,	,, ,,	*Ipse, ipsa, ipsum.*
El, la, lo	,,	,, ,,	*Ille, illa, illud.*

[2] The technical translation would be *¡No! no si se siente tan hambrienta* or *¡No! no si tiene tanta hambre.*

didn't come.' A. 'That's the very reason why I didn't.'
El miércoles fué fiesta pero no viniste. A. *Pues, por eso.*

An idiomatic and rather colloquial use of *eso* is *a eso de . . .*
meaning 'round about': *A eso de las 5*, 'Somewhere about
5 o'clock'.

espaciador (m). Space-key on a typewriter (*v.* OFF. APP.). Single
spacing, *a un espacio*; double-spacing, *a dos espacios*, etc.

espárragos (m. pl.). Always used in the plural and means asparagus (*v.* FOOD).

esperar. It seems extraordinary to us that a rich and expressive
language like Spanish should, by some curious mischance,
have only one word for 'to wait', 'to expect', and 'to hope'.
One may, of course, amuse oneself by inferring national
characteristics and talking wittily of a *Sala de Espera* as being
synonymously, in the Spanish mind, a waiting-room and a
hoping-room[1] but every language has its lacunae and the
Spaniards are well aware of subdivisions of meaning within
the word and have their own ways of indicating them.

One way is by the use of the verb *suponer* when the meaning
is 'I expect so' or 'I expect not': 'I expect so', *Supongo que sí*
and 'I expect not', *Supongo que no*. *Creer* may be used in the
same way. Most uses of the verb 'to expect' can be handled
in this way with a little ingenuity, e.g. 'I expect him to come',
Supongo que vendrá, or *Creo que vendrá*, thus disposing of that
aspect of the verb which implies waiting without any suggestion of emotion. Generally speaking, therefore, it can be
taken that *esperar* implies hope but the Spaniards tend to
give point to it by adding *sí* or *no*. *Lo espero* comes rather near
to meaning 'I expect so', whereas *Espero que sí* or *Espero que
no* makes it clear that definite hopes are intended.

As for waiting, the context usually makes this aspect clear:
Le esperaba en la esquina, 'She was waiting for him at the street
corner'. It should be borne in mind, too, that very often a
genuine compound of the three aspects is perfectly accurate,
e.g. when meeting a train, or indeed in the case of the lady at
the street corner above mentioned. A further translation of
the verb *esperar*, therefore, is 'to meet': *Voy a esperarle al
aeropuerto*, 'I'm going to meet him at the airport'. *Esperar*
is the proper word for 'meet' in this sense.

espinacas (f. pl.). Always used in the plural but means simply
'spinach' (*v.* FOOD).

espumadera (f). A 'spatula' for removing foam or scum (*v.*
DOM. APP.).

---

[1] It should not be forgotten that even in French, that proverbially precise and
logical language, both 'to wait' and 'to expect' are covered by '*attendre*'.

esquina (f). It means 'corner' but the *outside* of a corner, e.g. of a street; the inside type, e.g. of a room, is *rincón*, and you will need to make yourself conscious of the distinction which does not exist in English.[1] *La esquina* is the usual word for a street corner and if you spoke of *el rincón de las dos calles* it would be assumed that you must mean the corner of a square. Generally speaking *rincón* suggests indoors and *esquina* outdoors, though the Spaniards, like ourselves, may refer to *un rincón pintoresco de Sevilla* as 'a picturesque corner of Seville'.

estacionar. To park (*v.* CARS). A more usual verb is **aparcar** (*q.v.*). **estacionamiento** (m). 'Parking', 'car park'.

estar. If you are among those who find it difficult to distinguish between *ser* and *estar* (and which of us is not?) it may be useful to bear in mind that *estar* comes from the Latin *stare*, 'to stand', and to recall such phrases as 'Stands Scotland where it did?'[2] and 'I stand corrected'. If you know Italian you will know '*come sta?*', normally to be translated 'how is?' Spanish only carries this sort of thing a small stage further.

One translation of *estar* is 'to be present' and consequently the word may be used by itself in contexts where we feel the need of a preposition. On the telephone, when you want to say, 'Is Mr. So-and-So there?' you merely say in Spanish, *¿Está el Sr. Fulano?*:[3] 'It wasn't there' and 'He wasn't there' would be *No estaba* or *No estuvo*. You do not add the word *allí. Lo he buscado pero no está,* 'I've looked but it isn't there'.

este, -a, -o (*v.* under **eso**).

estera (f). A mat (*v.* DOM. APP.). (For doormat *v.* **felpudo**.)

estofado (m). Stew (*v.* FOOD).

estropajo (m). In so far as there is a Spanish word for 'dishcloth' this is it, but it is not in the least like a dishcloth, it is a sort of fibre of which you take a grubby little handful and claw at the dish like the gentleman in *Cold Comfort Farm*. Housewives who take pride in nice kitchen arrangements will usually find that Spain is no place for them, but there are big compensations; servants are plentiful and cheap and you need hardly ever enter the kitchen.

estupendo. Literally 'stupendous', but it equates with 'marvellous', 'terrific', 'gorgeous', and borders on slang therefore. An occasional use is permissible, but excess, though it make the unskilful laugh, cannot but make the judicious grieve (*v.* also **precioso**).

éxito (m). Rather a chestnut in the way of Falsos Amigos; you must be aware that it means 'success' and has nothing to do with the way out. Exit, *salida. Tener éxito* is the normal

---

[1] People who felt inclined to scoff about *esperar* can now think again; Spanish, in this case, is more subtle and precise than English.
[2] Macbeth, IV, iii.
[3] And the answer will be: *Sí está* or *No, no está* accordingly.

phrase for 'to be successful', 'to come off': *En el colegio tenía mucho éxito*, 'He got on extremely well at school'; *Lo intenté pero no tuve éxito*, 'I tried it but it didn't work'; *no sé si va a tener éxito*, 'I don't know whether it'll come off' (another, more colloquial, possibility for this is *No sé si me saldrá*).

Exito could often be translated 'popular': *Tiene mucho éxito con las chicas*, 'He is very popular with the girls'.

expedir. A False Friend, in a way, as it does not mean to expedite but simply to send off, to despatch: *Ya han sido expedidos*, 'They've been sent off already'. It is specially used in business letters (*v.* OFF. APP.). To expedite is *meter prisa*.

F

fa. F in MUSIC (*q.v.*). It cannot be applied to the subdominant.

facilitar. Something of a Falso Amigo since the commonest meaning is 'to supply', 'to let have': *Nos ha facilitado un coche*, 'He let us have a car', or 'He got hold of a car for us'. It is not merely colloquial, indeed it is probably commonest in business letters: *Mucho le agradecería nos facilitara . . .*, 'We should be most grateful if you would let us have . . .' (or 'supply us with . . .'). It does, however, also mean 'facilitate' and only the context will make matters clear; *Eso ha facilitado mucho las cosas*, 'That helped things a lot'.

factura (f). A 'bill' of the sort you have to pay (*v.* OFF. APP.); an invoice. In restaurants it is usually *cuenta*.

faisán (m). Pheasant (*v.* FOOD).

fallar. To fail, to fall short. I include it here in connection with playing cards where it means 'to fail to follow suit' (*v.* CARDS).

falta (f). An Unreliable Friend as it seldom translates as 'fault', nearly always as 'default': *El ascensor se paró por falta de luz*, 'The lift stopped for lack of current' or '. . . because the current went off'. *Por falta de* is a straight translation of 'in default of', though the latter is not necessarily the best translation. *Sin falta*, 'without fail'. You would, however, say *Hay varias faltas en la traducción*, 'There are various faults in the translation'.

A phrase which should be learned as a cliché is *No hace falta*, 'It is not necessary'. *Hacer falta* is one of the commonest ways of expressing necessity and *hace falta* is the equivalent—at any rate colloquially—of the French *il faut*. In English the translation tends to be complicated, but 'need' is one of the commonest equivalents: *Hace falta un martillo*, 'You'll need a hammer' (or 'I'll . . .' or 'We'll . . .', the personal pronoun often remaining unspecified), however, *No me* (*le, nos, os*) *hace falta*, 'I (we, you) don't need one' is common enough.

Another phrase which should be learnt whole is *No faltaba más* or *No faltaría más*. Literally this means 'No more was (or could be) wanted' but in practice it has come to be the polite way of saying 'Don't mention it' or 'Please do', and as Spaniards are often most vociferous in their thanks or apologies you should din it into yourself until the saying of it becomes almost a conditioned reflex. It is likely to be added instinctively to *Por Dios* (*q.v.*).

faro (m). Headlight of a car. Sidelights are usually referred to as *Luces* (*de estacionamiento*).

fastidiado. This borders on slang but it is really the English equivalents which are slangy; it means 'browned off', 'cheesed off', but is more polite than either of these. If you want to say 'bored stiff' it is probably a better word than *aburrido*, which tends to mean 'boring' rather than 'bored', but it is to be hoped that you will not need it at all. *Fastidio* is the noun and *¡Qué fastidio!* is a common way of saying 'What a nuisance!', 'How irritating!'

¡Fastídiate!, literally 'get annoyed about that!' is the Spanish equivalent of the childish 'So there!'

favor, haga el favor, haz el favor. 'Excuse me', 'Do you mind?' and used when you are about to do something which will cause inconvenience, e.g. getting out of a crowded tram. The phrase should be learned off pat and substituted for the word which, I suspect, comes most readily to your lips, viz. *Perdone. Perdone,* like *Excusez-moi* in French, is an *apology* for an inconvenience caused, *not* a request when you are about to cause one, and is therefore incorrect on the latter occasion.[1] *Haga el favor* is the introduction to any polite request, e.g. *Haga el favor de traer mi equipaje*, 'Will you be good enough to fetch my luggage', or *Haga el favor de darme sus señas*, 'Will you give me your address?' *¿Quiere Vd. darme sus señas?* means rather 'Would you like to give me your address?' but the distinction is not always important in practice.

felpudo (m). A door-mat made of coconut fibre (*v*. DOM. APP.).

feo. An extremely common word which means the opposite of 'nice' and therefore according to context, 'nasty', 'unpleasant', 'ill-mannered', 'not done' (though this would often be *Mal visto*), 'indecent', 'coarse', 'in bad taste', etc. A little boy wiping his nose on his sleeve would be told by a bourgeois mama *Eso es muy feo*, 'That's not at all a nice thing to do'. 'Not nice' is probably the best basic concept.

---

[1] A person will hear you say *Perdone* and fail to move because he imagines you are addressing, not him, but the man behind on whose toe you have just trodden (*v*. **perdone**).

When applied to persons, however, it means simply 'ugly', and is therefore the direct antonym of *bonito* which means 'nice' for things and 'pretty' for people. *¡Es un tío tan feo!*, 'He's such an ugly fellow!' and it contains no unavowed suggestion that the man is not nice: *Es simpática pero un poco fea*, 'She's nice but rather ugly'.

fiambre (m). A general word for cold meats including brawns, pâté, salamis, etc. (*v.* FOOD).

fianza (f). A deposit, of the type you pay to your landlord, usually for the amount of one month's rent.

ficha (f). This curious word occurs very often and has several different meanings. One is approximately 'counterfoil' *not* of the sort you leave in your cheque-book, which is *una matriz* but a 'slip of paper' which you detach and put on the file for record purposes; it is also, therefore, the individual 'card' in a card-index (*v.* OFF. APP.). Another meaning is the dummy coin which, in Spanish public telephones, you put in the slot instead of pennies (or nickels). The telephones are usually in cafés or shops and you buy the *ficha* at the counter. (The price of telephone calls can thus be raised without difficulty.) It is also a chip, counter, marker, domino.

fichero (m). A card-index, meaning the whole piece of furniture containing it (*v.* OFF. APP.).

figura (f). Most often it means simply 'figure' but I include it here as, in connection with playing-cards, it means a face card (*v.* CARDS).

fijarse. 'To apply oneself', 'to concentrate on', 'to pay attention to'. Its commonest colloquial use is in the expression *¡Fíjese!* or *¡Fíjate!* which means 'Just think!', 'Just imagine!'. This exclamation is particularly common in ladies' conversation.

filtro (m). Filter, here included in connection with CARS (*q.v.*).

flan (m). A False Friend, in its way, as it is not any sort of fruit tart but simply caramel custard or egg custard. It is one of the commonest Spanish *postres* (*v.* FOOD).

flauta (f). Flute (*v.* MUSIC).

flecha (f). Literally arrow, here flipper, direction-indicator (*v.* CARS).

fogón (m). Stove, kitchen-range. It is still common in Spanish kitchens and provides the only available oven and must be heated by the good old-fashioned method (mostly scrappy bits of wood). Gas stoves complete with oven are not yet universal in Spain and you will need a good deal of experience before you are able to cook a decent pie (pastry is, therefore, likewise little known, except in shops and restaurants). Gas is laid on in many houses in the big cities but often it serves only a gas-ring or a brace thereof.

formal. Another Amigo Informal. It can mean 'formal', e.g. *Hacer una petición formal*, 'To make a formal application' but unless the context indicates such a meaning it signifies 'reliable': *Es un chico muy formal*, 'He's a very reliable fellow' (also *un chico de mucha formalidad*).

fracaso (m). *Fracas* in French and we often use the same word in English. The essential meaning in Spanish is 'wash-out', 'muck-up', but it is not slangy, nor even merely colloquial. *La fotografía fué un fracaso*, 'The photograph was a wash-out'.

frambuesa (f). Raspberry (cf. Fr. *framboise*) (*v.* FOOD). It is not a very common fruit in Spain as a whole, though in the north-west conditions are more appropriate for the cultivation of soft fruits.

fregadero (m). The usual word for 'sink' (*v.* DOM. APP.). The word *pila* (*q.v.*) is frequently used, but this also could be applied to a 'sump' or the like[1] whereas *fregadero* means strictly the place where the washing-up is done. It derives from the verb:

fregar. To wash up (*v.* DOM. APP.).

frenar, freno (m). 'To brake' and 'brake', respectively (*v.* CARS). *Un frenazo*, 'jamming on the brakes', 'braking'; *freno de mano*, 'hand-brake'; *freno de pie*, 'foot-brake'.

fresa (f), **-ón** (m). *Una fresa*, 'a wild strawberry' (Fr. *fraise du bois*). *Un fresón*, 'strawberry' of the usual cultivated sort (*v.* FOOD); (mech.) drill, bit, milling tool.

fresco, frescura (f). Literally 'fresh', but frequently applied to persons, when it means 'cool' in the sense of 'cheeky': *Es un poco fresco, ¿verdad?*, 'He's a bit cool, isn't he?' *Frescura* is the usual noun for 'cheek': *¡Qué frescura!*, 'What cheek!' though *impertinencia* may also be used (*v.* also **caradura**).

frito, -s. As an adjective it means simply 'fried', but as a noun, in the plural, it means small fish snacks fried in batter and served as *aperitivos* (*q.v.*), e.g. *calamares* (*q.v.*), sardines, etc.

fuente (f). A dish of the oval sort on which food is normally served. Generally speaking it suggests a largish one and it would be the translation of the Scottish 'ashet'. It is not used metaphorically to denote the food itself (*v.* DOM. APP.).

fuerte. As you know, it means 'strong', but in music it is more likely to mean 'loud' (*v.* MUSIC).

Fulano. A fictitious name similar to our John Doe and Richard Roe but equating more with 'Mr. So-and-So' or 'Smith, Jones and Robinson', as it is very common. One reason for its commonness is probably the Spanish love of recounting stories very much in *oratio recta*, with all spoken remarks quoted verbatim and all noises imitated onomatopœically (e.g. *pam, pam, pam*, or *paf, paf, paf*, which can indicate

---

[1] *Pila* can also mean other quite different things, e.g. 'pile', 'dry battery', etc.

somebody walking upstairs or firing a gun or any other repetitive noise you please) and, of course, with a wealth of excited gesture. People who tell stories in this way are continually confronted with the need to specify a person's name and *Fulano* fits all circumstances. The English, on the whole, tend to prefer *oratio obliqua*, but most of us have met the type who refers frequently to 'John Smith' in the course of his stories. If he were a Spaniard he would say *Fulano* and if he required further personages (i.e. Jones, Robinson, etc.), they would be *Mengano, Zutano and Perengano*, in that order. If even more are needed then diminutives are resorted to, i.e. *Fulanito, Menganito*, etc.

If you are anxious to emphasise the 'Mister' part of it you would say *El Señor Fulano de Tal* as *Fulano* by itself tends to suggest a Christian name rather than a surname. When referring to a woman care must be used to include her title: e.g. *La Señora Fulana de Tal*, since *una fulana* means 'a whore'.

fusa (f). A demi-semiquaver in MUSIC (*q.v.*).

G

galleta (f). Biscuit. And beware of *bizcocho*, which means sponge-cake.

gallina (f). Strictly 'hen' but here you may read it as 'chicken' (*v.* FOOD). *Un gallina* (m) is a somewhat slangy word for a coward (cf. chicken-hearted).

gamba (f). Prawn (*v.* FOOD). As indicated under **mariscos**, the Spaniards are connoisseurs of shellfish and the *gamba* is the prototype. By English standards the prawns are large, but they range from small to enormous and there is a different word for nearly every size:

Quisquilla (f). Shrimp. In comparison with *gambas* these are uncommon, probably because they are such a fiddling nuisance to peel.

Gamba (f). Prawn. These are all but universal.

Langostino (m). A huge prawn. They taste slightly sweeter. They should not be confused with the French *langoustine*, which the Spanish call:

Cigala (f). I do not know the English word for this creature, in fact I do not think we have one as it does not, I believe, occur in home waters. It is like a small, pink and very elongated lobster and has a most prehistoric, crustacean appearance. A pair of nut-crackers is needed to deal with the shell of the pincers though fingers may be used at a pinch (or a prick) for the main body. They are very similar to *langostinos* in flavour.

Cangrejo de río. Crayfish or crawfish.
Cangrejo. Crab, but less common than in the north.
Langosta. Lobster.
For other popular sea-foods, *v.* **almejas, boquerones, calamares, percebes.**

gamuza (f). A shammy (*v.* DOM. APP.). A bit of old cloth used as a duster would be referred to as *Un trapo* (*q.v.*).

ganar. To win, at games, battles, etc. (*v.* CARDS).

ganas de, tener. To want to, to feel like (Fr. *avoir envie de*). *No tengo ganas*, 'I don't feel like it'; *¿Tienes ganas de ir al concierto?*, 'Do you feel like going to the concert?'

garaje (m). Garage (*v.* CARS).

garbanzo (m). This is a bean of the haricot type (i.e. the seed) but rather more rotund. It is a common ingredient of a stew and, being cheap, is widely eaten but does not seem popular with more refined palates.

gas (m). Gas, as in English (*v.* DOM. APP.).

gasolina (f). Petrol (Amer. gas) (*v.* CARS).

gato (m). Cat, of course, but, in connection with cars, a 'jack' (*v.* CARS).

gemelos (m. pl.). The proper word for 'twins', but also the name given to 'cuff-links' (*v.* DOM. APP.).

genial, genio (m). *Genial* is a Falso Amigo as it means 'having genius', 'of genius', and has no connotation of the English word 'genial' which would have to be translated *cordial, sociable*, or *cariñoso. Es un compositor genial*, 'He's a genius of a composer' or 'He's a genius' simply. Mentioned more because of its falsity than because you are likely to need it.
   Genio you are more likely to need, and it is likewise false. *Es un genio* does mean 'He's a genius' but *Tiene genio* means 'He has temperament', and *Es un chico de mucho genio*, 'He's a very quick-tempered chap', and is often a polite way of saying 'bad tempered'. *¡Qué mal genio!*, 'What a nasty temper!' The root concept is somewhere near 'quick on the draw' (or 'trigger', if you prefer).

gente (f). People, in the general sense, and it is important to remember that it takes a singular verb since in English we say 'People *are*'. *En invierno la gente va a la Sierra*, 'In winter people go to the mountains' (i.e. for ski-ing); *Había mucha gente*, 'There were a lot of people there'. If you wanted to say, 'What a crowd!', however, you would say *¡Qué gentío!* since *¡Qué gente!* signifies 'What awful people!'
   Gente menuda, 'small fry', i.e. lesser people.
   As you know, it is not the only word for 'people'. 'The Spanish people' is *El pueblo español* and *el pueblo* means 'the common people' as opposed to the aristocracy and bourgeoisie.

giro postal. Postal order would be a reasonable translation for this but the Spanish procedure is not the same as ours. When you wish to send somebody some money you go to the post office but you do not receive the order in exchange and send it yourself, you pay the money and give the full name and address of the person to whom you wish it to be sent, receiving in exchange simply a receipt for the money. The post office sends the money and the recipient at the other end will in due course receive the money or, if the amount is rather great, a note informing him that there is some money waiting for him and will he please come and get it. Usually he may send a *Cobrador* duly empowered to collect it on his behalf.[1]

Giros postales may not be negotiated through banks and indeed the British banking system is virtually unknown throughout the continent of Europe. Banks in Spain exist chiefly for such purposes as loans and mortgages, and not only do private individuals not have bank accounts but many business firms do not have them either.

To make matters more difficult, one is not allowed to send money in an ordinary letter through the post; it is not merely a matter of 'owner's risk'. If you want to send money in a letter you have to use the *Valores declarados* system.

gracia (f), **gracioso, -a.** Another interesting evolution from the original Latin *gratia*. In the Spanish mind the essential concept is amusement, wit. *¡Qué gracioso!* is the most usual way of saying 'How witty!', 'How amusing!' (though see also **divertido**). It would be sufficient to say simply, *¡Qué gracia!*, 'What wit!', 'How witty!', 'Isn't it amusing!', or *Tiene mucha gracia*, 'It's very amusing'. It is something of a Falso Amigo as it does not mean 'gracious', which would have to be *cortés* or something similar.

granada (f). Pomegranate, so called from its place of origin, though the fruit is probably more cultivated in the Levant nowadays. *Granadina* is the juice (Fr. *grenadine*); it is bright red, very sweet and sold in bottles for flavouring drinks or (for children) diluting with *sifón*.

grapa (f). Paper-fastener, i.e. of the two-prong sort which you divide once the paper is penetrated (v. OFF. APP.).

grasa (f). Grease (v. CARS).

grave. It may mean 'grave', i.e. 'serious', but in music it means 'low', 'deep' (v. MUSIC). *Una nota grave*, 'A low note'; *Una voz grave*, 'a deep voice'.

grifo (m). Tap (v. DOM. APP.).

grosella (f). Red currant (v. FOOD).

---

[1] The maximum amount that can be sent by one *giro postal* is 5,000 pts. (about £50; July 1951). For greater amounts you must either send several *giros postales* or a *giro telegráfico* for which the amount is unlimited.

guapa (adj., f). Probably the commonest word for 'pretty', hence my putting it in the feminine form.

In the entry under **piropo** you will will find a reference to *¡Guapa!* which is one of the commonest of such compliments. It can also be used directly to a young lady whom you know slightly, e.g. *¡Hola, guapa!*, 'Hello, beautiful!' or *¡Adiós, guapa!*, 'Good-bye, beautiful!' and although such remarks indicate a desire to know the lady better and are in any case a little familiar, they are not quite as cheeky as they sound in English. It is a convention in Spain to pay exaggerated compliments to women, though I know no country (I only know Europe) where their status is more definitely inferior, and if you accompany your *¡Adiós, guapa!* with a special look and a little hand-squeeze, you are most unlikely to get your face slapped. On the other hand you are likely to get very little else. A Spanish woman may receive compliments *ad nauseam* but she is not expected to return them, and even if you do get the tiniest little squeeze back you should not allow it to raise your hopes unduly high. There is nothing doing with Spanish women unless you intend marriage and even then it is a family affair and a formal contract. Spanish sexual conventions are very oriental and based on the brothel, these institutions being regarded as a means of keeping decent women pure. Implicit in this is the tacit assumption that no male is to be trusted alone with a young female for more than a minute or so and this has the curious result that if he *is* so left he often does not feel the need to be trustworthy. Another, more serious, result is that although there is any amount of lasciviousness there is comparatively little love, since young people of opposite sexes have little opportunity of getting to know one another as human beings on an ordinary, decent footing. The emancipation of women has certainly raised problems in the countries where it has been adopted but this old-fashioned system just as certainly has its problems too. However, when in Madrid do as the Madrileños do, say your *¡Guapas!* and enjoy your hand-squeezing but do not read too much into it.

guardabarro (m). Mudguard, fender (*v.* CARS).

guinda (f). A black cherry (*v.* FOOD). A white or red cherry is *cereza* (*q.v.*).

guión (m). Literally guide, and used where we might say 'book of words', in reference to some explanatory brochure. It is also the current word for hyphen or dash in typing (*v.* OFF. APP.). It is not the universal word for guide; telephone guide (i.e. directory), *guía telefónica*; a 'railway guide' is likewise *una guía* (*de ferrocarriles*).

Guión is also the usual word for 'script' (motion pictures, radio, etc.).

guisantes (m. pl.). Peas (i.e. green peas) (*v.* FOOD). The flowers 'sweet peas' are called *guisantes de olor*.

H

¡hablar, ni! This indicates a very strong, though perfectly polite, negative and therefore equates with 'Good heavens, no!', 'Not a bit of it!', 'No fear!', 'I won't hear of it!', 'Certainly not!', 'Nothing doing!', etc. Q. *¿Te ha dado el dinero?* A. *¡Ni hablar!* Q. 'Did he give you the money?' A. **'Certainly not!'**, **'Good heavens, no!'** In English we tend to prefer understatement, and if somebody offered us something which we considered undesirable we should probably reply with a rather stiff 'No, thanks!' but in Spanish they express themselves more fully, e.g. Q. 'Do you want a ticket for the bull-fight?' A. 'No, thanks!' Q. *¿Quiere ir a los toros?* A. *¡Ni hablar!* ('I certainly do not.')
A milder form of *¡Ni hablar!* is *¡qué va!*

hacerse. One of the words for 'become'. *Se ha hecho bastante popular,* 'It (or he) has become pretty popular'. For other translations of 'become', *v.* **convertirse, pasar.**

hacer caso (*v.* **caso**).

hacer falta (*v.* **falta**).

hacha (f) (although *el hacha* in the singular). Literally, hatchet, but used colloquially to mean a most effective, clever person. *Eres un hacha,* 'You're terrific!'

haga (haz) el favor (*v.* **favor**).

harto de, estar. 'To be fed up with', 'to be sick of', *Estoy harto de esperar,* 'I'm sick of waiting about'. It is distinctly colloquial but not in the least vulgar.

hasta. As you know, it means 'until' in relation to time and 'as far as' in relation to place, but it is used in such a multitude of occasions when these translations would not be used in English that this is clearly the moment to consider the whole problem of leave-takings, since that is when it most occurs. As indicated earlier in this book, *Adiós* is the universal word for 'Good-bye', but it is seldom used by itself unless to greet a person *en passant* and without stopping to say more; always, apart from this, something is added. In ordinary formal relations with strangers it would simply be *¡Adiós, buenos días!* or *¡Adiós, buenas tardes!* but if there is any possibility of a further meeting then *hasta* is attached and its significance is more subtle than might be supposed, so I list them:
Hasta ahora is used when the second meeting will be almost at once and is a common ending to a telephone conversation.
Hasta luego is not quite as quick but suggests that the next meeting will be on the same day.
Hasta mañana obviously indicates that the next meeting will be on the next day and presupposes a definite knowledge

to that effect; it is not said regardless. You say it to the colleagues you work with and if it is a Saturday morning and you will not see them till Monday then you do not say it, you say *Hasta el lunes*.

Hasta pronto has more of the pious wish about it. It does not specify a time very accurately but does contain a hope that the next meeting may not be long delayed, so it is usually rather cordial.

Hasta la vista is a little less cordial and even less precise. It is by no means rude but it is slightly more familiar. It is the nearest to the French *au revoir* and the concept is certainly 'till we meet again'—whenever that may happen to be— (if you know then you state it and therefore do not say *Hasta la vista*).

Hasta siempre is extremely friendly, even affectionate, and means in effect 'Whenever our next meeting may happen to be you will be more than welcome'. You would only use it to an established friend when taking a long leave of him (or her).

This does not exhaust the list since particular circumstance or individual fantasy may indicate others, or coin them at will, but I think it covers all the commoner ones and should suffice to remind you that, when speaking Spanish, even so simple a word as 'good-bye' may require a good deal of quick and careful thought.

hay que. This is a general and impersonal way of indicating necessity, rather like the French *il faut*; in English it is hard to manage without a pronoun: *Hay que coger el tren de mediodía*, literally 'It is necessary to catch the midday train', but in practice we should say, 'They'll have to . . .', or 'We'll have to . . .', etc., according to circumstances. *Hay que cuidarse*, 'You've got to be careful'; *Hay que vivir*, 'One's got to live'; *Hay que seguir esperando*, 'We shall have to go on waiting'. If you have to specify the person for whom the necessity arises you would use *tener que*: *Pepe tiene que irse*, 'Joe's got to go'.

helado. As an adjective it means 'iced', e.g. *café helado*, 'iced coffee'. It is, however, frequently used as a noun and *un helado* means 'an ice-cream'.

higo (m). Fig, the generic name. The early black ones are called *brevas* (*v.* FOOD).

¡hijo! Without the exclamation marks, as you know, it means 'son' but with them it means 'my good boy' or 'you sweet guy' or 'you doll' or 'my dear chap' according to the relationship to the person to whom it is addressed and the tone of voice in which it is said. It indicates either familiarity or condescension, bearing in mind that condescension on the part of a senior to a junior does not necessarily count as such. Messenger-boys (*botones*, and they are common in Spain) are likely to be called it twenty times in the course of one day's work. Within such relationships it can be quite kindly—the equivalent of the English 'son' or 'sonny'—but with another tone of voice it can be extremely contemptuous and mean 'You silly little fool!' Quite common is *¡Pero hijo . . .!* accompanied by a wide gesture; no further word is needed to indicate that the person addressed has said (or done) something either ridiculous or outrageous, but in spite of that it is frequently followed by voluble explanations.

The feminine *¡hija!* is, *mutatis mutandis*, similarly used.

hilo (m). Wire.

hinchar. To pump (*v*. CARS).

¡hola! It is what you say when you meet somebody you know quite well and as often as not it is followed immediately by *Buenos días* (*tardes*, etc.). It is not necessarily familiar and is used with *Vd.* at least as often as with *tú*; it does, however, suggest a certain equality of status and you would not normally use it to a person much older than yourself unless it were a relative or someone equally intimate. The best equivalent is probably 'Hello!' Between colleagues at an office, 'What cheer!' and just as 'What cheer!' is usually followed by a Christian name, e.g. 'What cheer, Bob?' so is *¡Hola!* e.g. *¡Hola, Pablo!*

¡Hola! is really a little more respectful than 'What cheer!' (See also note under **olé**.)

¡hombre! I never imagine Spaniards in conversation but I seem to hear this exclamation on their lips. One might call it the most typical word in the Spanish colloquial vocabulary, as it expresses their characteristically animated response to what they are told but its very typicality makes it uncommonly difficult to translate into Anglo-Saxon terms. It may be said in emphatic or enthusiastic confirmation, in mild or indignant protestation or in contemptuous refutation. Usually other words follow and *pero* frequently precedes. *¡Hombre, ya lo creo!* is a cliché and worth learning; it usually means something like 'I should say so!' (Amer. 'I'll say!') or 'It certainly is (does, has, etc.)!', 'Rather!', 'Yes, indeed!', etc., i.e. in confirmation of something just said. In contemptuous refutation *pero* is likely to precede it, e.g. *¡Pero hombre! ¡ni hablar!* Any astonishing piece of information certainly demands *¡hombre!* as a response, e.g. *¡Hombre! ¡No me digas!* Mild protestation is likely to be handled by *¡Pero hombre . . .!* with no further words but an appropriate gesture with the arms, for this we might say 'But my dear man . . .!' or 'My dear fellow . . .!' though such expressions in English belong rather to the educated classes whereas *¡Hombre!* is universal.

Exclamations such as 'Good heavens!' or 'Good Lord!', used in the above contexts are about as near as we are likely to get to it but it is hopeless to try to learn the word as a translation of anything; one must simply learn to pop it in when responding animatedly to a surprising piece of information or to statements with which one heartily agrees or disagrees.

A milder form of it is *¡anda!* (*q.v.*). There are several stronger forms but they come outside my terms of reference, being distinctly vulgar. *¡Hombre!* is not in the least vulgar but it is essentially colloquial.

honesto. A Falso Amigo; its chief meaning is 'chaste' and consequently it is likely to occur more often in the feminine (cf. 'He made an honest woman of her').

'Honest' would normally be translated *honrado* (*v.* also *de confianza*).

honor (m). An honour in bridge (*v.* CARDS).

horno (m). Oven (*v.* DOM. APP.).

hoy día, hoy en día. Nowadays, in these days. One is sometimes tempted to use this expression when one means 'this very day' for which the proper translation is *este mismo día.*

huevos (m). Eggs (*v.* FOOD). A full Spanish menu includes an egg course which follows the soup or hors d'œuvres and precedes the fish. An omelette (*tortilla*) is often the choice but eggs may be done in a multitude of other ways and I give some of the most common:

(*Huevos*) *al plato,* shirred .
duros, hard-boiled.
escalfados, poached.
flamencos, fried in a little earthenware dish along with diced meat, etc. (this will be about the only occasion that you get a hot plate in Spain).
pasados por agua, soft boiled.
revueltos, scrambled.
rusos, Russian, i.e. what we usually call 'egg mayonnaise'. This is really a foreign importation and you will only come across it in rather cosmopolitan restaurants.
a la . . . (usually followed by the name of the restaurant). This is, of course, rather a shot in the dark and you must either trust your luck or, if you feel up to it, interrogate the waiter and hope that you will understand his replies. In my experience it is most often some form of *flamenco,* which, despite its name (Flemish), is a very Spanish way of cooking eggs.

I

ignorar. A Falso Amigo. Like the French *ignorer* it means 'not to know', 'to be unaware'—*Ignoro sus señas*, 'I don't know his address'; *Ignoraba que ella le quería*, 'He didn't realise that she was fond of him'. It can, of course, be used negatively and *No lo ignoro* is quite a good translation of 'I'm not unaware of it'.

The Spanish for 'to ignore' is *no hacer caso*, i.e. 'to take no notice (v. **caso**).

igual, igualmente. Very similar to the French *égal* though it ranges a little wider. *Es igual*, 'It's all the same', 'It makes no odds', 'I don't mind'. It is not always the best way of saying 'It does not matter' since it tends to mean 'Couldn't care less' if attached by the context to a personal pronoun; 'It doesn't matter' is most politely rendered by *No importa*. Frequently the equation is 'the same': *igual que antes*, 'same again' (in a bar often just *¡Igual!* with a descriptive gesture). *Igualmente* is 'the same to you', e.g. in reply to *Feliz Año Nuevo, Felices Pascuas*.

importar. To matter. More common than *importer* in French and not inelegant as it may be in that language. *No importa*, 'It doesn't matter'; *¿Qué importa?*, 'What does it matter?'[1] *Claro, esto importaba mucho*, 'Obviously that was an important point'. It is useful for conveying the English 'mind': *¿No te importa traerme un paquete de pitillos?* 'Would you mind bringing me back a packet of cigarettes?'

Another translation of 'to mind', used subjectively, is *no venir mal*: *No me vendría mal algo de beber*, 'I wouldn't mind a drink'; *No te vendría mal un baño*, 'You could do with a bath' (v. **venir bien**).

inclusive. Literally 'including' and therefore 'besides', 'moreover', but used so often in conversation that it often comes to mean 'even'. (The right word for 'even' is, of course, *incluso*.)

indicado. It means 'indicated' but is used a great deal in the purely adjectival sense and has come to mean 'likely', 'probable', 'obvious': *La elección más indicada*, 'The most obvious choice'.[2] It probably occurs most often in the comparative or superlative and the translations 'better' and 'best' are then nearest the mark: 'A pencil would be better than a pen', *Un lápiz sería más indicado que una pluma. Esto es lo más indicado*, 'That's the best thing'.

indicador (de velocidades) (m). Speedometer (v. CARS).

[1] Though *¿Qué más da?* is probably commoner for 'What does it matter?'
[2] Strictly speaking it should be: . . . *la más indicada*, but the article is usually omitted in practice.

ingenioso. An Amigo Informal; it does not mean 'ingenious' except when applied to such things as dialogue or ways of talking; the equation is, therefore, 'witty'. 'An ingenious person' would be *Una persona lista*. 'An ingenious idea', however, would be *Una idea ingeniosa* (or *feliz*).

inquilino, -a. Tenant, i.e. the occupant of a house or flat and therefore likely to be yourself.

intentar. Your grammar-book should have covered this and if I presume to mention it, it is chiefly to remind you that there is more than one word for 'to try' in Spanish. This one means 'to attempt', 'to have a go at', 'to try on'. If you mean 'to try *out*', 'to put to the proof', *v.* **probar.**

inventario (m). Inventory. Note that it is spelt with an 'a'.

ir, irse. See under **va, vámonos, vaya, voy.**

J

jaleo (m). A row, a brawl, an uproar. The basic concept is a 'mix-up' but it carries with it the suggestion of noise. In many contexts *lío* (*q.v.*) could be used instead but *lío* is basically a 'tie-up' and is more strictly figurative (and has therefore no suggestion of noise). *Un jaleo* really is the word for 'brawl', e.g. in a café or the street and the metaphorical meaning of 'confusion' is secondary. 'Row' is the best equivalent: *Hubo un jaleo enorme*, 'There was an awful row', and both in English and Spanish it could be a literal or metaphorical one.

jamón (m). Ham (*v.* FOOD). Usually rather half-smoked and tough in Spain.

jaula (f). Literally cage, but it can apply to almost any cell in which something can be locked up and therefore equates with a 'lock-up garage' (*v.* CARS).

jerez (m). Sherry. In the past our ancestors made a more valiant attempt to pronounce the word fully and in the seventeenth and eighteenth centuries it was often called 'Sherries'. *Jerez* covers all the types of wine produced in the vicinity of Jerez de la Frontera, from the lightest and driest *Tío Pepe* to such heavy-sweet liquids as *Pedro Jiménez*. On the whole the Spaniards much prefer the light sorts and most often ask for *manzanilla* (*q.v.*).

¡Jesús! As indicated in the entry under *Dios*, Spaniards are not inhibited about using the names of sacred personages for a variety of unsacred purposes, but this one is never used as an impious exclamation as it is in the United States or Ireland or, to a lesser extent, in Britain; it is simply the conventional thing to say when anyone sneezes. In the old days the English used to say 'Bless you' (it lingers still in places) and just as the phrase was short for 'God bless you' so *¡Jesús!* is short for *¡Jesús te asista!*

The conventional and automatic response, usually gasped into a handkerchief, is *Gracias*.

judías (f). Literally Jewesses, but the ordinary word for 'green beans'.

juego (m). Literally game, but in bridge it does not mean 'game' but 'rubber' (*v*. CARDS).

juerga (f), **juerguearse.** This is a difficult word to translate; *juerga* is an enthusiastic bout of wining, dining and 'womanising', in company. *Correrse la gran juerga*, 'to go on the tiles' (cf. Fr. *faire la noce, faire la bombe*); *Nos hemos corrido la gran juerga anoche*, 'We had a hell of a party last night'. 'Orgy' might do.

jugar. To play, in nearly every sense of the word except to play a musical instrument, which is *tocar*. Here included for card players (*v*. CARDS).

L

la. A, in MUSIC (*q.v.*). It cannot be used to mean the super-dominant.

lámpara (f). Lamp, yes, but also electric bulb, though *bombilla* is more precise (*v*. DOM. APP.).

langosta (f). Lobster (*v*. FOOD).

langostino (m). A sort of large prawn (*v*. entry under **gamba**).

largo. Such a classic Falso Amigo that perhaps I insult you by mentioning it; it means 'long', not 'large' (as in English) nor 'wide' (as in French and Italian). It is fatal to remember '*Largo al factotum*' even if the Barber did come from Seville. 'Wide' in Spanish is *ancho* or *amplio*. 'Large' is *grande* or again *amplio*; 'long' is *largo*.

lata (f). As indicated under **bote,** this properly means a tin (Amer. can) of preserved food, but for some reason which is hard to explain it has come to take on the metaphorical meaning of 'nuisance': *¡Qué lata!*, 'What a nuisance!', *Es una lata*, 'It's a bore'. *Dar la lata* means 'to make oneself a nuisance', 'to molest': *Estaba dando la lata como siempre*, 'He was making a nuisance of himself, as usual'. Another, rather more serious, word for nuisance is *molestia*.

lavabo (m). As in French it means simply a wash-basin, i.e. of the sort fixed to the wall (*v.* DOM. APP.).

lechal. An adjective from *leche*, milk, which, applied to animals, equates to 'sucking'. *Cordero lechal*, 'sucking mutton', i.e. 'lamb'. For 'sucking pig', however, *v.* **cochinillo**.

lechuga (f). Lettuce (*v.* FOOD).

lectura (f). A Falso Amigo; it means 'reading'; *La lectura de la Biblia*, 'The reading of the Bible'; *Sala de lectura*, 'Reading-room', 'A lecture' is *Una conferencia*, another False Friend.

legumbres (f). Vegetables, but of the dry sort, e.g. *garbanzos* (*v.* FOOD). For green vegetables, *v.* **verdura**.

lejía (f). A name given to a solution of chloride of lime which is widely used in Spain for cleaning purposes. A favourite trick of lazy laundresses is to put it into the washing water, with the result that the clothing comes out beautifully white but disintegrates within a few months, so if you keep house in Spain keep an eye on your *chica*'s use of *lejía*.

lenguado (m). Sole, i.e. the fish (*v.* FOOD).

lento. The usual word for slow in a musical context and outside it (*v.* MUSIC).

liarse. Very colloquial but extremely common; it means 'to start doing something and keep on doing it', so that 'to get stuck into', 'to get weaving', 'to get down to', 'to wade in' are possible equivalents. It takes *a*: *Se lió a hablar y no paró en una hora*, 'He got down to talking and didn't stop for an hour'.

ligas (f. pl.). 'Suspenders' in the English sense, i.e. for socks or stockings. For suspenders (English 'braces') in the American sense, *v.* **tirantes**.

limón (m). Lemon.
   (*v.* FOOD).

limpiaparabrisas. Windscreen-wiper (*v.* CARS).

lío (m). As indicated under **jaleo** (*q.v.*), this is a common word meaning a 'tangle' though it can be used more strictly in the sense of binding (see next paragraph). The American expression, 'It's a mixup' would be *Es un lío. Había un lío tremendo en la Puerta del Sol* would suggest there was a 'traffic jam', a 'muck-up', whereas *un jaleo tremendo en la Puerta del Sol* would suggest a riot.
   Another use of it concerns a 'tie-up' between two individuals, i.e. an affair of the heart. *Tiene un lío en su oficina* would mean 'He's courting a bit of stuff in his office', i.e. he's got something that ties him to his office, though this would not be immediately understood unless the context had made it clear.

líquido de frenos (m). Brake fluid (*v.* CARS).

listo. Hardly my business but worth having at your tongue's tip as you often want to say 'I'm ready' or 'Are you ready?' which are *Estoy listo* and *¿Está(s) listo?* respectively. The meaning 'ready' only applies with the verb *estar*; with *ser* it means 'clever', *Es un chico muy listo*, 'He's a very clever chap'; *Es listísimo*, 'He's frightfully clever'. If you are not careful you may find yourself saying *hábil*, which can also be translated 'clever' but means rather 'clever with one's hands' so that 'skilful' would be a better translation.

loza (f). A general word for 'earthenware', though objects made of it are likely to have names of their own (*v.* DOM. APP.).

lubina (f). Call it 'halibut' since it is more like halibut than any other fish in British waters, though it is usually served rather differently. It is extremely good (*v.* FOOD).

luego. Mentioned in order to warn you off *entonces* (q.v.) in cases where the latter either will not do or is not so idiomatic. Both words mean 'then' but *luego* brings in the sense of sequence. If you were recounting a story to children and paused at an exciting moment they would say to you *Y ¿luego?*, 'And then . . .' but it is by no means confined to children, and the Spanish for 'What happened then?' or 'What happened after that?' or 'So what?' is in most cases simply *Y ¿luego?* *Entonces* tends to mean 'in that case' whereas *luego* means rather 'at that point'. Sometimes the translation would be 'next' used adverbially (not adjectivally, which would be *próximo* or *otro*). 'First she went to the grocer's, next to the butcher's, and then to the hairdresser's' would be *Primero fué a la tienda, luego a la carnicería y después a la peluquería. Luego* often means 'afterwards' or 'later': *Lo haré luego*, 'I'll do it afterwards' and *luego* by itself, 'later', 'in a moment', 'afterwards'.

For *desde luego* and *hasta luego, v.* **desde** and **hasta** respectively.

lumbre (f). Fire, usually with reference to the fire in the kitchen stove since open fires are not common in Spanish houses. The most common colloquial use of the word is in reference to 'light' for a cigarette: *¿Tiene lumbre?* 'Have you got a light?' *¿Tiene luz?* would not be permissible for this though *¿Tiene fuego?* would. The verb 'to light' is, of course, *encender*.

luz de estacionamiento (f). Sidelight, parking light (*v.* CARS).

LL

llamada (f). A call on the telephone. A long-distance call, however, is *una conferencia* (q.v.). **llamar,** 'to ring up'.

llave (f). Key, ignition key, wrench (*v.* CARS).

llegar (a ser). One of the renderings of 'become' in the sense of 'turn out': *ha llegado a ser evidente que . . .*, 'it has become obvious that . . .'. An adjective is required after *ser*; you cannot say *ha llegado a ser que . . .* to mean 'it has turned out that . . .'. This would have to be *ha resultado que . . .* (*v.* **resultar**).

llevar. The usual word for 'to take' in the sense of to take along with you. I mention it here chiefly in connection with music, e.g. 'I'm going to take this at two in a bar', *Voy a llevar esto a dos* (*v.* MUSIC).

M

maleta (f), **maletín** (m). *Maleta* is the usual word for a suit-case; *maletin* is a small suit-case. *Valija* (valise) is not used except in special cases, e.g. *valija diplomatica,* diplomatic bag sent from embassies.

mande, mándeme. Sometimes used by a waiter or shop-assistant instead of *dígame* when requesting your order. It means simply, 'Yes, sir?' (literally 'order me'). You are unlikely to need it yourself but it is as well to recognise it when you hear it.

manera (f). Perhaps the commonest equation of 'way', e.g. 'in this way', *de esta manera*; 'It wasn't a very nice way of doing things', *Fué una manera un poco fea de hacer las cosas. De manera que,* 'so that'.

maneras, de todas. One of the commonest expressions for 'any-way', 'whatever happens', 'in any case', 'at all events': *De todas maneras vendré a la una,* 'Anyway, I'll come at 1 o'clock'; *Vendrá esta tarde de todas maneras,* 'He'll be coming this evening whatever happens'. Other, equally common expressions, are *de todas formas* and *de todos modos* (*v.* also *por lo menos*).

It is possible to say *en todo caso* but this suggests rather 'in every case' and one of the above is more likely. (If you meant 'in every single case' you would say *en cada caso.*)

manga (f). Means a number of rather diverse things, e.g. 'sleeve', 'hose-pipe', 'beam' (i.e. width of a ship), etc. I include it here as in bridge it means 'game' (*v.* CARDS. For 'rubber', *v.* **juego**).

mango (m). Handle, in nearly all senses (*v.* DOM. APP.). *Un mango de escoba,* 'a broomstick', and in Spanish, too, it has its associations with witches.

manivela (f). Cranking-handle (*v.* CARS).

mano (f). Hand, of course, but in cards it refers to the person whose lead it is: *¿Quién tiene la mano?*, 'Whose lead is it?' (*v.* CARDS).

mano de almirez. A pestle (*almirez*, 'mortar') (*v.* DOM. APP.).

manta (f). Blanket, rug, i.e. what you put on a bed or take in a car (*v.* DOM. APP.).

manteca (f). Lard . In Andalusia it is often used instead of *mantequilla*, and means butter.

mantel (m). Table-cloth (*v.* DOM. APP.).

mantequilla (f). Butter .

manzana (f). Apple (*v.* FOOD). It is also the word for a block of buildings, e.g. *Vive a dos manzanas de aquí*, 'He lives two blocks away from here'.

manzanilla (f). A kind of light, white dry sherry from Sanlúcar de Barrameda, though it does not strictly count as sherry. I do not know the derivation of the name but the drink is certainly not made from apples. It is perhaps the most popular of all short drinks at a bar and commonly accompanied by *tapas* (*v.* FOOD).

máquina (f). Machine, of course, but frequently short for *máquina de escribir* and therefore 'typewriter'. *Máquina de direcciones*, 'addressograph' (*v.* OFF. APP.).

marcar. To mark, in the general sense, but in connection with telephones it means 'to dial a number' (*marcar un número*) (*v.* TELEPHONES). In bridge it means 'to bid' (*v.* CARDS).
   Una marca is a 'make' or 'brand' of manufacture, e.g. *Es la mejor marca de coche que hay*, 'It's the best make of car there is'.

marcha atrás (f). Reverse (*v.* CARS).

mareado. *Marea*, 'tide', but *mareado* is a common expression for 'sea-sick', 'giddy', 'tight', 'half-seas-over', etc., and often just plain 'sick'. 'Sick' is the proper translation; the meanings connected with drunkenness are slangy.

mariscos (m). Sea-food, shellfish.[1] It is a remarkable fact that Madrid, though it is at no point less than 200 miles from the sea, and about 400 miles from Corunna where most of the shell-fishing is done, is better supplied with fresh and excellent shellfish than probably any other European capital, and the same, *mutatis mutandis*, is true of most other Spanish towns. In England, apart from the odd shrimp, I confess I hardly thought about shellfish in the past, and the inclusion of the word *mariscos* at this point is a measure of the extent to which I have become persuaded of their worthwhileness. I have therefore discussed the different varieties in comparative detail and enthusiasts, actual or potential, are referred to the entry under **gamba.**
   Certain cafés—usually called *Cervecerías*, as beer is the normal accompanying drink—specialise in *mariscos* and there

   [1] Beware of *morisco* which means 'Moorish'.

an enthusiast can really go to town; you wade in through prawn-shells two inches deep, either to a table or to the counter, and there proceed to add to the mess on the floor. Plates are provided for the shells in case you should wish to be more refined about it, but in such an *ambiente* it seems a little out of place and there is a certain unbuttoned pleasure in recklessly using the floor. Apart from these, practically any bar or café is likely to have *gambas, almejas, boquerones*, or other delicacies, and I have never heard of anyone suffering through eating them.

marreco (m). A counter in card games; it is worth five *tantos*.

martes trece. 'Tuesday the 13th'; I mention it because it is the Spanish equivalent of Friday the 13th in England, i.e. it is supposed to be an unlucky day.

martillo (m). Hammer (*v.* CARS, DOM. APP.).

más allá. Further on (*v.* **allí, allá**).

más bien. 'Rather', when something is being more correctly stated (Fr. *plutôt*): 'He shut the door—or rather he tried to', *Cerró la puerta—o más bien lo intentó.*

matrícula (f), **-arse.** A Falso Amigo: *matricular* means 'to register' (something) and *matricularse* therefore means 'to register oneself', i.e. to enrol. *Matrícula*, 'Registration number' (or card) and in connection with cars it therefore means 'licence plate' (*v.* CARS). There is no proper Spanish equivalent of our 'matriculation' as their educational system is different.

mayonesa (f). Mayonnaise (*v.* FOOD).

mayor. Not only 'greater' and 'larger' but also 'older' and 'elder': *su hermano mayor*, 'his elder brother'. It may also mean 'major', e.g. *la mayor parte*, 'the major part', and it certainly means 'major' in MUSIC (*q.v.*). It is not, however, the Spanish for the field rank of major, which is *Comandante*.

mecanógrafo, -a. A typist (*v.* OFF. APP.).

mechero (m). Cigarette lighter. It is possible to say *encendedor* but it sounds very pedantic, and *mechero* is the universal word, even though it borders on slang.

mediante (f). Mediant (*v.* MUSIC).

medias (f. pl.). Stockings.

medio, por término. It might have seemed more consistent to put this under **término** but **medio** is the operative word; it means 'middle', 'medium', 'mean', 'average', and *por término medio* 'on the average'. There is really nothing colloquial about it, but it is surprising how often the word 'average' is used by this scientifically and statistically minded generation and I suspect you are likely to need it.

mejor, a lo mejor. Obviously, it means 'better' but it is used a lot by itself meaning 'It'd be better' or 'I think that would be preferable' or 'That's more like it!' according to one's tone of voice. *A lo mejor* is perhaps even more common and in most contexts the translation would be 'probably', though the literal meaning is 'at best'. Q. *¿Cree que vendrá?* A. *A lo mejor, sí.* Q. 'D'you think he'll come?' A. 'Probably', 'I expect so', 'I think so'; *A lo mejor vendré a la una*, 'I'll probably come at one o'clock' or 'With any luck I'll be there by one o'clock.' *Probablemente* does exist and it is not uncommon, but if you want to be more authentic about your Spanish I recommend *a lo mejor* in its place. (And if you think your Spanish is already pretty authentic how would you translate *A lo mejor no me sale.* For answer, see **salir**.)

melocotón (m). Peach, but of the cling variety, i.e. a deep golden yellow but rather turnipy when eaten raw, and in some ways nicer when tinned (*v.* FOOD).

menor. Minor, both in the sense of 'younger' (e.g. *hermano menor*, 'younger brother') and in the musical sense (e.g. *Sol menor*, 'G minor') (*v.* MUSIC).

menos, por lo menos, menos mal. Like its cousin *mejor*, *menos* is often used alone: *Sí, pero menos* is 'Yes, but not so much', 'Rather less so', but used more often than we should use these English expressions.

Por lo menos is very common and is most useful as an equation of 'anyway', though its strict meaning is 'at least'. *Por lo menos vendré yo si es posible*, 'Anyway, I'll come if I can'; *Tiene por lo menos quinientas mil pesetas*, 'He's got at least half a million pesetas'. Generally speaking the translation is 'anyway' unless *por lo menos* immediately precedes an amount of something. If you mean 'Anyway, he's got half a million pesetas' it would be *Por lo menos tiene* as opposed to *Tiene por lo menos*.

Menos mal, another common expression, appears to mean 'not so bad', but it is said in a different tone of voice, viz. one of relief, and the best equation is 'Thank goodness!' If, after a run of bad luck at a game of cards, your opponent at last leads the suit you wanted you exclaim, *¡Menos mal!* Again, if someone has been ill and you now hear better news of his state you say likewise *¡Menos mal!* 'Oh, good!' would often be the translation.

menta (f). Mint (*v.* FOOD). It is far less common than in England.

menudo, a. Frequently, often. It contains a suggestion of irregularity: *Viene aquí a menudo*, 'He often comes here' (but you never know when).

merecer. To be worth or to be worth while, and similar to *valer* but capable of taking a greater weight. The concept is manifestly 'to merit'. *No merece la pena*, 'It's not worth while' (though probably in the negative *No vale la pena* would be commoner) but if you want to use it positively, i.e. 'it's worth it', 'it's worth a try', you would say *lo merece* (or *merece la pena*); if you said *lo vale* it would suggest that it is worth it merely in terms of money.

merluza (f). Haddock (*v.* FOOD).

mermelada (f). Jam, not marmalade, which is called *compota*.

mero (m). A kind of Mediterranean bass for which we have no real name (*v.* FOOD).

mesa (f). A table, as you know, but normally used in offices where we should say 'desk' (*v.* OFF. APP.).

meter(se). One of the many equations of 'to get', this time in the sense of 'get into'. 'Get into bed!', *¡Métete en la cama!*; *¡Métete en lo que te importe!*, 'Mind your own business!' If you want 'get out' then a different verb is needed, such as *sacar* or *salirse*. 'Get out of bed!' would be *¡Salte de la cama!*[1]

People sometimes ask what is the difference between *meter* and *poner*. The answer is: in practice often very little, but in so far as there is, *meter* is 'to put into' and *poner* is 'to put on' or 'put out'.

There are several more particular uses of *meterse*, one of the commonest being 'to poke one's nose into', 'to meddle' and so 'to interfere' (*v.* also **dificultar**): *Siempre se está metiendo en los asuntos de los demás*, 'He's always poking his nose into other people's business'; *Ella se mete en todo*, 'She interferes in everything'.

A further meaning is 'to tease' and then it takes *con*: *A ella le gusta meterse conmigo*, 'She likes teasing me'.

mi. E, in Music (*v.* MUSIC).

micrófono (m). In addition to the usual meanings of microphone, this is used where we should say 'mouthpiece', i.e. of a telephone.

miedo (m). Literally fear, as you probably know; *¿Tiene miedo?* is straightforward Spanish for 'Are you afraid?' Just as in English we extend the basic notion of fear to words like 'fearful', 'frightful' and 'awful', however, so do the Spanish extend *miedo*. *Era una cosa de miedo*, 'It was simply ghastly'; *Es de miedo*, 'It's awful'.

miel (f). Honey (*v.* FOOD).

minuta (f). Menu, bill of fare (*v.* FOOD). (When masculine, it means a minute.) The word *menu* can also be used and it is about the only one you will hear in elegant restaurants.

mismo (lo). As you will know by now, *lo* is the remains of the Latin neuter *'illud'* and the result is that the adjective attached

---

[1] I use the 2nd person singular but it could be used in the 'polite' form too. An uninvited guest who has insisted on staying, not only the night but late in bed, could be told *¡Sálgase de la cama!*

to it can stand by itself. In French, if you wanted to say to a waiter, 'Same again', you would have to say *La même chose*, but in Spanish you can say simply *Lo mismo*; if you start *el mismo* (i.e. the Latin masculine) then some masculine noun must follow, e.g. *el mismo día*. Clearly *lo* can be, and is, attached to many other words besides *mismo*, e.g. *Lo mejor sería que tu vinieras conmigo*,[1] 'The best thing would be for you to come with me', and *lo mejor*, meaning 'the best thing', is worth learning as a cliché. So is *lo mismo*; both are very common, and you should warn yourself off *el mismo* standing by itself.

A common expression is *Me da lo mismo* which would appear to mean 'It's all the same to me' (cf. Fr. *Ça m'est égal*) but it is not so callously indifferent as the English and is not so much 'I don't mind' as 'I don't mind in the least'. Tone of voice, however, is important; you could say *me da lo mismo* in such a way as to leave no doubt that you could not care less.

mitad (f). You know this as meaning 'half', like the French *moitié*, e.g. *Me dió la mitad*, 'He gave me half'; but you may not know it as also meaning the French *milieu*, e.g. *en mitad de*, '*au milieu de*', 'in the middle of' even in the physical sense: *En mitad de la arena lo mató*, 'In the middle of the bull-ring he killed it' (or 'it killed him' according to context);[2] or *En mitad de la conversación se calló*, 'Half-way through the conversation he shut up'.

modos, de todos (*v.* **de todas maneras**).

modulación (f). Modulation, change of key (*v.* MUSIC).

molestar, molestia. This is the sort of word that reminds us that English is basically an earthy Germanic language; for us 'molest' is used a little specially and, on the whole, is an 'educated' word whereas for Spaniards it is basic and used any number of times a day. It therefore equates with such words as 'bother', 'trouble' and 'nuisance': *No se moleste* is the normal way of saying 'Don't bother', 'Please don't trouble' (applying particularly to putting oneself out in a physical sense, e.g. getting up to open the door: 'Don't bother your brains about it' would more probably be *No se preocupe*). *¡Qué molestia!* equates with 'What a nuisance!' (though *¡Qué lata!* is more colloquial) and *Me temo que le estamos molestando*, 'I'm afraid we're making ourselves a nuisance'. 'Trouble' in the physical sense could often be *trabajo*, 'He had a lot of trouble getting tickets', *Le costó mucho trabajo conseguir entradas* (for a concert).

[1] Classical scholars may be interested to know that the *-go* at the end of *conmigo*, *contigo*, etc., is the remains of the Latin *'cum'* in *'mecum'*, *'tecum'*, etc. To say *contigo*, therefore, is really redundant as it is putting a 'with' both before and after the pronoun. This explains, however, why one does not say *sinmigo*, *sintigo*, *paramigo*, etc.

[2] Though *en medio de* would be more likely unless you particularly wished to stress the half-way point. *En mitad de* is perhaps rather 'Right in the middle of'

molinera (f). A 'miller's wife' but as in French (*meunière*) it is applied to that particular method of cooking fish (*v.* FOOD).

¡**mona**! I put it in the feminine because that is by far the commonest form; it is something like *guapa* (*q.v.*) but I have not heard it used as a *piropo* (though I dare say it is). It seems mostly to be used between women when greeting one another and the best translation is therefore 'My dear!' My secretary, who was continually being rung up by her girl friends, used invariably to greet them with ¡*Hola, mona!* and it would be ridiculous to translate it, 'Hello beautiful!' 'My dear! How are you?' would be much nearer the mark, though the difference in national temperaments results in a good deal of difference of intonation.

It is not used only as an exclamation. It is perfectly in order to describe a nice-looking girl as *muy mona*.

The noun *mona* means a female monkey but the adjective, surprisingly enough, means 'polished', 'elegant', 'beautiful'. There is no connection with the English Christian name 'Mona' which comes from Erse and means 'noble'.

mora (f). Blackberry (*v.* FOOD).

mordente (m). Strictly speaking a mordent (⌇) in music but used somewhat laxly to mean a grace-note (*v.* MUSIC).

mostaza (f). Mustard, but it will be the French type. The highly piquant sort used in the British Isles seems to be almost unknown elsewhere (*v.* FOOD).

moto (f). The current abbreviation for *motocicleta* hence 'motor-bike' (*v.* CARS).

motor (m). The engine of a car, not the car itself (*v.* CARS).

movido. Animated, fast, especially in MUSIC (*q.v.*).

muelle (m). Spring, of the spiral type (*v.* CARS). For the laminated type, *v.* **ballesta.**

muerto (m). Literally dead, but it is the name given to dummy in bridge (*v.* CARDS).

multicopista (m). Duplicator, duplicating-machine (*v.* OFF. APP.).

N

nabo (m). Turnip (*v.* FOOD).

nada, de. This should be one of the first clichés you ever learn. It means, of course, 'Don't mention it', 'Not at all', but is used far more often than even these expressions in English, being the automatic and almost unconscious response to the word *gracias* (cf. the German *bitte* in response to *danke*). It is true that the Spaniards do not say *Gracias* quite so often as we say 'Thank you' or 'Thanks', but they say it pretty often, nevertheless, and *de nada* follows like a conditioned reflex, so be sure and condition yours.

Nada se pierde is a cliché meaning 'There's no harm done', 'All's well', 'No bones broken', 'Everything's all right', etc.

naipe (m). The proper Spanish word for playing-card, though it is being rapidly replaced by *carta*.

naranja (f). Orange (*v.* FOOD).

nata (f). Cream (usually whipped); **natilla,** custard (*v.* FOOD).

natural. Natural in all senses, including musical (♮) (*v.* MUSIC).

naturalmente. Mentioned chiefly to suggest that you avoid saying it. It is true that 'naturally' in English, being helped out by 'obviously', 'of course', and the like, is less common than *naturellement* in French and *natürlich* in German, but so many people approach Spanish through a French or German haze, or else think of their Latin, that they find themselves saying *naturalmente* when they would be better saying *desde luego* or *claro*. *Naturalmente* does exist but it has more the meaning of 'in the course of nature'; it is also used in formal manners of speech and in letters; you will be understood if you say it but *desde luego* is far more idiomatic.

negra (f). A crotchet (cf. Fr. *noire*) (*v.* MUSIC).

neumático (m). Do not be disconcerted by the spelling; it means a 'pneumatic' and, therefore, a 'tyre'; it has nothing to do with medieval musical notation. It applies to the whole tyre, inner tube and outer casing combined; the outer casing by itself is called the *cubierta*, and the inner tube the *cámara* (*v.* CARS).

nevera (f). Literally 'snower' and, therefore, a refrigerator or an ice-box (*v.* DOM. APP.). The word *frigidaire* is also used for the electric type.

ni siquiera. 'Not even', and rather stronger than *ni aún*, which, however, is not incorrect: 'I couldn't even raise a loan from my brother', *Ni siquiera mi hermano me ha querido prestar dinero*. 'I shan't be going to the cinema; I haven't got enough (money) even for the tram', *No voy al cine porque ni siquiera tengo (dinero) para el tranvía.*

buenas noches. 'Good night', obviously, but 'Good evening', too, and not quite as simple as it seems; it is a greeting as well as a parting. Spaniards, for their part, have difficulty in remembering that 'good night' can only be said on parting and will sometimes disconcert you by shaking you warmly by the hand and saying 'good night' on arrival.

nulos (m. pl.). Misère (*v.* CARDS).

O

oboe (m). Oboe (*v.* MUSIC).

octava (f). Octave (*v.* MUSIC).

oficina (f). An office in the general sense; an individual's private office would be referred to as a *despacho* (*v.* OFF. APP.).

¡oiga! As indicated in the Preface of this book, Spaniards use the imperative with far less compunction than we do and *¡Oiga!* is one of the commonest of imperatives. It means literally 'Listen!' but people who habitually say 'Listen!' in English are not, as a rule, well thought of and it sounds rude. In Spanish it does not; it is said a hundred times a day and the equations are therefore numerous. One of the commonest is on the telephone, where it means 'Hello?' or 'Are you there?' when the conversation is being taken up again after a break (not when you first answer; that is *Diga* (*v.* TELE-PHONES) though many Spaniards will shout it into the mouthpiece every time a new idea comes into their heads.

Another occasion on which you use it is when you want to attract attention, e.g. when you go into a shop and there is no one behind the counter, so one equation is 'Shop!' De la Mare's traveller, if he had been a Spaniard, would have said simply *¡Oiga!* instead of 'Is there anybody there?' thus ruining the whole poem. *¡Oiga!* is, of course, the polite form and the intimate is *¡Oye! Tenga la bondad de* (infinitive) is another common imperative.

These abrupt imperatives are not really so rude as they seem, since they are very often followed by *por favor* but it is to be noted that their English equations are nearly always in the form of questions, e.g. *Espere un momento, por favor*, 'Will you hold on a moment?'—and I confess that I think the greater sensibility indicated by putting it in interrogative form reflects a difference in civilisation.

¡olé! It is chiefly an ejaculation of appreciation and encouragement contributed by the spectators of a *flamenco* song or dance. If you have gramophone records of these entertainments you will probably find a few *Olés* included. *Flamenco* singers find it almost impossible to perform *in vacuo* and need an audience even more than comedians in B.B.C. studios, so that it is usual to include them for a gramophone recording. I have referred to them as 'spectators' but the word is not ideal, the relationship with the performer being quite an intimate one. The most typical gatherings are in small rooms, usually with all doors and windows shut and a thick haze of cigarette and *manzanilla* fumes. The singer and his guitarist are in amongst the audience and there is none of our tendency to be embarrassed when meeting the performer's eye; on the contrary the singer and one of his hearers are likely to be staring at each other's faces about a foot apart, the singer's eye piercing some remote place beyond the listener's skull and the listener gazing intently back, nodding encouragement and getting more and more excited. When at last the singer, inspired by this encouragement, achieves some more than normally cadenza-like arabesque and finally brings the music to its inevitable Phrygian cadence there is immediately a *tutti* of *¡Olés!* from all present to round it off. It is not necessary to wait until the end, however, before uttering the word; if the music excites you sufficiently you will ejaculate *¡Olé!* at any time, just as a believer is provoked into an occasional 'Alleluia' in the middle of a prayer at a revivalist meeting.

It is interesting to note that both *Hola* and *Olé* come from the Arabic and are none other than our old friend Allah in disguise. *Hola* may be equated with *a Dios* which, as explained under **adiós,** can be a greeting simultaneous with a parting. *Olé* comes from the Arabic *'w'Allah'* meaning *por Dios* (*v.* **Dios**). In other words when you exclaim *Olé* at a *flamenco* session you are in effect ejaculating 'My God!'

olla (f). This, perforce, has to be translated 'saucepan' but it is not of a type we normally use in Great Britain. Its size varies and it has two little handles, one each side, but as they are usually made of aluminium, like the pot itself, you will still have to take a cloth or two in order to pick it up off the stove as the handles will be too hot to hold. It frequently does service as a kettle since this phenomenon is little known in Spain, but if you are not careful the *olla* which cooked your stew for lunch will be used to heat the water for your tea and the consequent taste of onions or garlic will be all too conspicuous.

Oporto (m). The town in Portugal but also port wine (oporto).

ordinario. A Falso Amigo. It does *not* mean 'ordinary', although it would be possible to think up contexts where the two could equate; it means 'common', 'vulgar', 'rude'. *Es un chico muy ordinario,* 'He's a very rude boy'. If you wish to stress the commonness rather than the rudeness you would say *mal educado* (cf. the expression 'ignorant' often used by the British working classes to indicate the same thing); the Spanish word for 'ordinary' is *corriente, regular* (*q.v.*).

As a noun, *ordinario* means a transport agency, though the usual word for this is *recadero* (*q.v.*). Compare the English 'common carrier', which equates almost exactly.

oros (m). Approximately diamonds, but it applies only to Spanish playing-cards and is not applicable to ours where the word is *diamantes* (*v.* Note, p. 141).

ostra (f). Oyster.

otro. This means not only 'other' but 'another' and thence 'one more', 'again' and 'next'. 'Again', admittedly, is *otra vez*, but means 'one more time' and if it were 'one more kiss', e.g. 'Kiss me—and again!—and again!' the Spanish would be '*Dame un beso—¡otro!—¡otro!*, not *un otro*. The meaning 'next' applies when *otro* is used with the article, and can mean 'next' both in a forward and a backward direction; thus, if you are driving a car along the street and are uncertain whether the next *bocacalle* is the one you want you say *¿Es ésta?* and if the reply is *No, la otra*, it means 'No, the next one', but if it were '*No, era la otra*, it would mean 'No, it was the last one'; in other words it means 'next' or 'last' according to the context and the tense of the verb. *El otro día*, however, means simply 'the other day' not the previous day', and 'next Monday' is more likely to be *el lunes próximo*.

P

paella (f). One of the most typical and popular of Spanish dishes, though you often have to order it half an hour beforehand. It is a sort of kedgeree, rice being the main constituent. The other matter is not merely little bits of fish but large lumps of fish, chicken, shellfish, or what you will; you frequently get clams, crawfish, etc., in their shells and are then obliged to get them out, so it is no use hoping to keep your fingers clean.

palanca (f). Handle, but included here because, in a car, it is short for *palanca de cambio*, i.e. gear-handle or gear-lever (*v.* CARS).

palier (m). Axle-shaft (*v.* CARS).

palmatoria (f). Candlestick (*v.* DOM. APP.). Perhaps it sounds rather romantic but it is such a common phenomenon for the lights to fail in Spain that all householders will be wise to keep a *palmatoria* and a *vela* or two handy in the house (or rather flat).

palo (m). A general word for 'stick', though it may also mean 'handle', e.g. *el palo de la escoba*, 'the broomstick'. It also means a 'suit' at CARDS (*q.v.*). **palillo** (m) is the word applied to the little pointed sticks with which you spear olives, anchovies, and the like.

pan (m). Bread, yes, but *un pan* (Fr. *un pain*) means a full-sized loaf of bread. Other sizes have other names, e.g. *barra*, *bollo* (*q.v.*).

panel (m). Means 'panel' in the widest sense, but is sometimes used for 'splashguard'.

pantalones (m. pl.). Trousers.

papel carbón (m). Carbon paper (*v.* OFF. APP.).

papel secante (m). Blotting paper, but usually referred to simply as *secante* (*v.* OFF. APP.).

parabrisas (m). *Parasol*, as your grandmother knew, means 'against the sun' and *paraguas* means an umbrella, so by a simple logical process you can readily deduce *parabrisas*, 'windscreen', and *limpiaparabrisas*, 'windscreen-wiper'.

parachoques (m). Bumper (*v.* CARS).

paraguaya (f). A peach, somewhat of the type grown in England, i.e. with pale green flesh, but slightly flattened top and bottom (*v.* FOOD). The other type of 'peach' is *melocotón* (*q.v.*).

parar. To stop, including to stop the engine, therefore 'To switch off' (*v.* CARS).

parecer. A very common verb for which the straightforward meanings of 'seem' or 'appear' are valid in most contexts. Bear in mind, however, the English word 'like' in expressions such as 'to look like' which would usually be translated by *parecer*. 'He looks like a foreigner', *Parece un extranjero*; 'It looks rather funny', *Parece un poco raro*. The 'like'-ness is, of course, not confined to looking but can equally be smelling, tasting, sounding, or any of the other senses: if, on descrying some object in the distance you said *Parece una bomba* a Spaniard would probably understand you to mean, 'It looks like a petrol pump', but if you made the same remark after hearing a loud bang in the distance it would mean 'It sounds like a bomb going off'. The basic concept is, therefore, 'to be like'.

One or two clichés are worth learning by heart: *Me parece que sí*, 'I think so'; *Me parece que no*, 'I don't think so'. *Parece mentira* is a common expression which should not be taken at its face value; it does not mean 'It sounds like a lie' except in a very remote and literal sense and the normal equation is more like 'Would you believe it?', 'Isn't that extraordinary!' or 'You'd hardly credit it', or just plain 'No!' in an incredulous tone of voice.

Another very common cliché is *¿Qué te* (or *le*) *parece?*, 'What d'you think?', 'What's your opinion?', 'What have you got to say to that?', 'How d'you like that?'

parecido is the usual word for 'similar'. *Algo parecido*, 'Something like that'; *Una cosa muy parecida*, 'Something very similar'; *Eran muy parecidos*, 'They were much alike'.

paréntesis (m). A bracket in writing (*v.* OFF. APP.). *Entre paréntesis*, 'in brackets', but it is used quite often in ordinary speech where we should say 'by the way', or 'incidentally', i.e. when going off at a brief tangent.

párrafo (m). A paragraph, i.e. the complete set of lines. When dictating you do not say *párrafo* when you mean her to start a new paragraph, you say *punto y aparte* (*q.v.*).

parrilla (f). A grill, i.e. the iron bars on which the food is cooked (*v.* FOOD). A grill in the sense of the bars that screen a window is *una reja*.

pasar, pase, etc. *Pasar* is one of the words for 'to become' as well as the commonest word for 'to happen'. *¿Qué pasa?*, 'What's happening?' 'What's going on?'; *a veces pasa que . . .*, 'it sometimes happens that . . .'

 ¡Pase! means 'Come in!' in an answer to a knock at the door, though a better expression for this is *¡Adelante!* (*q.v.*). If you are being ushered in or out of a door then *¡Pase Vd.!* is likely to be the exclamation, and if the exit coincides with someone else's and you are standing upon the order of your going, then *¡Vd. primero!*, 'After you'.

 paso ('I pass') is the normal expression for 'pass' or 'no bid' at CARDS (*q.v.*).

pasas (f. pl.). Raisins (*v.* FOOD). It can be applied to other fruit besides grapes, e.g. *ciruelas pasas*, 'prunes'.

pasta, pastel. *Pasta* means paste, and can be applied to the sort of paste one sticks papers together with; in connection with food, however, it has the same meaning as in Italian, i.e. a generic name for the macaroni family—spaghetti, vermicelli, noodles, etc.

 pastel, cake and *pasteles*, cakes.

 pastelería, 'pastries', though pastry as we know it is not common in Spain, except occasional flake pastry in cakes, etc., and bought in shops. It is very seldom made at home (*v.* FOOD).

patata (f). Potato (*v.* FOOD).

patinar. Literally to skate, but in a car, to skid (*v.* CARS).

patinazo (m). The noun for a skid (*v.* CARS).

pato (m). Duck (*v.* FOOD).

pavo, pavipollo (m). Turkey (*v.* FOOD).

pedal (m). Pedal (*v.* both MUSIC and CARS).

pegar. To stick (i.e. with glue) but the usual colloquial word for 'to hit', 'to strike', 'to swipe', 'to sock'. *¡Pégale!*, 'Hit him!', 'Sock him one!' It borders on slang but you will find it almost universally used. If you want a more correct expression use *dar un golpe*.

peine (m). Comb.

pelea (f). A quarrel, squabble, row. **Pelear,** to squabble, to row. It is a little colloquial but cannot be called slangy.

pelo, tomar el. Literally 'to pull (one's) hair', but metaphorically 'to pull (one's) leg': *Me está tomando el pelo*, 'You're pulling my leg', *No le tomes el pelo*, 'Stop pulling his (her) leg'.

pena (f). Trouble, misfortune, sorrow. If you know French then it equates almost exactly with *peine*, *No vale la pena*, '*Ça ne vaut pas la peine*', 'It's not worth the trouble' or simply 'It's not worth it'.(You could also say *No merece la pena*.)*¡Qué pena!*, 'What a shame!', 'What a pity!' *Le causó mucha pena*, 'It was a great sorrow to her'.

pendientes (m. pl.). Ear-rings.

pentagrama (m). Stave, in MUSIC (*q.v.*). Obviously it refers to the five lines.

pera (f). Pear (*v.* FOOD).

percebes (m. pl.). A sort of barnacle. They have such a nightmarish, surrealist aspect that those who do not know them will feel most disinclined to eat them when they see them, but they nevertheless have enthusiastic supporters who swear they are the best sea-food going. For my own part I confess I find them rather unexciting and hardly worth the labour and nuisance of eating but it is entirely a matter of taste, perhaps of acquired taste.

perdiz (f). Partridge (*v.* FOOD). It is quite a common bird in Spain and therefore quite a common dish in restaurants.

¡perdone! This is an apology, like the French *pardon*, and the English for it is therefore 'I'm sorry!' or 'I'm so sorry!' or just 'Sorry!', according to circumstances. It is not the proper equivalent of the English 'Pardon me' or 'Excuse me', which is not an apology so much as a request when you are *about* to do something inconvenient; for this the Spanish is *Haga el favor* or *Haz el favor*. It is, however, the equivalent of the American 'Pardon me' when something has not been understood and you are asking for it to be repeated.

perejil (m). Parsley (*v.* FOOD). The plant is much longer and lankier in Spain.

pescado (m). Fish (*v.* FOOD). A good many Spanish varieties, being fished from more southern waters, have no exact equivalent in English, e.g. *lubina*, *mero*. In other cases we have a word, though the fish is not a home product, e.g. tuna fish, bonito, sardine, swordfish. Some, however, occur in both countries, e.g. sole (*lenguado*), turbot (*rodaballo*), haddock (*merluza*), plaice (*platija*), herring (*arenque*).

pichón (m). A young pigeon and the usual word for pigeon on the table (*v.* FOOD). The bird itself is usually called *una paloma* (dove), but 'pigeon-shooting' is *tiro de pichón*.

y pico. 'And a bit' or 'odd', in connection with numbers: 'My father is fifty odd', *Mi padre tiene 50 años y pico*; *A las seis y pico*, 'Sometime after 6 o'clock'; *Setenta pesetas y pico*, '70 pesetas and a few odd céntimos'; *Catorce y pico*, '14 and a bit'.

If, however, you are referring, say, to the 1930's you would not say *los treinta y pico*, you would say *los treinta y tantos* (*v.* **tantos**).

piloto (m). Pilot, but also pilot-light, hence tail-lamp (*v.* CARS).

pinchazo (m). Puncture, referring to CARS (*q.v.*). You might have expected it to be *punctura* but no such word exists in Spanish. The Spanish derivation from the Latin *punctum* is *punción*, which is a medical word, e.g. *punción lumbar*, 'lumbar puncture'.

¿a qué pinta? A cliché for 'What's trumps?' (*v.* CARDS).

piña (f), **Piña de América** or **Ananás.** Pineapple (*v.* FOOD).

piropo (m). This phenomenon has been touched on under **guapa** and it is something for which we have no word so we have to do the best we can with 'compliments'. It is by no means unknown in England for workmen, soldiers, and the like to shout 'compliments' at young women who happen to be walking past, though more often than not the 'compliment' is merely a long-drawn-out whistle. The Spaniards are more readily articulate in such matters and may call out anything from *¡Chata!* or *¡Guapa!* to long and flowery phrases, more or less poetically worded, and the convention of doing so has become so accepted that they have a word for it, viz. *piropo*. Sometimes the phrases are quite prettily turned but in other cases they are unblushingly outspoken and obviously, whether well or badly done, they all hinge on the bedworthiness of the lady concerned.

Since you, reader, may well be a young lady, it is more than probable that in your visits to Spain you will have *piropos* shouted at you and it is therefore right that you should know how to react in such circumstances. In a certain sense, of course, you must not react at all; you must continue straight ahead, looking neither to the right nor the left and making a very obvious show of paying no attention. Be sure, however, that it is obvious; really to appear not to have heard is almost insulting to the man and may waste a good *piropo*. There is no need to look indignant, even if the *piropo* is a fairly stiff one; after all no woman really minds being thought desirable. If the *piropo* is quite a polite one you may allow your features to draw into a half-smile but you must on no account look at the man who made it (and it will not always be a workman; it may very well be a respectably dressed, middle-aged man at a café who looks as though he ought to know better). If you are walking with another lady then you may even, if the *piropo* is respectable enough, allow yourselves to start giggling together once past the scene of the crime. This will be much appreciated and no danger attaches. If, however, the *piropo* is rather high, or *verde*, as a Spaniard would say, then danger does begin to attach if you react too favourably.

Clearly you would like to be given some examples of *piropos verdes* but it would be impossible to begin, so wide is the range, and in any case they fall outside the scope of this book. And it is perhaps just as well you should not understand them since, if you did, you might burst out laughing there and then with worse than fatal results.

I am told that the calling out of *piropos* is far less common than it used to be and is virtually on its way out. It is for you to decide whether you are pleased or sorry about this.

pisapapeles (m. s. pl.). Paperweight (*v.* OFF. APP.).

piso (m). Literally a 'floor' or 'story', e.g. 'a ten-story building', *un edificio de diez pisos*; 'they lived on the fifth floor', *vivían en el quinto piso* (*planta* is also ground floor, e.g. *trabajo en la planta baja*). In practice, however, it has come to mean a 'flat': *Le invité a mi piso*, 'I invited him to my flat'.

The floor of a room, as seen from the inside, is usually regarded as the 'ground', e.g. 'It fell on the floor', *Cayó al suelo*.

pisto (m). A very Spanish dish, being a sort of hash composed of marrow, pimento, beans, and other odd vegetables hashed up together and fried in olive-oil (*v.* FOOD). Personally I like it very much.

pistón (m). Valve of a brass instrument (*v.* MUSIC). Also piston in engineering (*v.* CARS).

pitillo (m). A colloquial but almost universal word for cigarette and similar, therefore, to our erstwhile 'fag' and 'gasper'.

plan de, en. In this form the best translation is probably 'as if' or 'just as if': *Salieron en plan de novios*, 'They went out together (for all the world) as if they were engaged'. If you use *en plan* without the *de*, however, another translation is necessary, e.g. *Si lo haces en ese plan*, 'If you do it in that sort of way'. The basic concept is 'as if'.

plancha (f). An iron for laundry purposes. **planchar,** 'to iron' (*v.* DOM. APP.). It is sometimes used for a grill: *gambas a la plancha*, 'grilled prawns'.

platija (f). Plaice (*v.* FOOD).

platinos (m. pl.). Contact-points (*v.* CARS).

plato, -illo (m). *Plato*, 'plate', and may also be used metaphorically to mean 'dish' (i.e. the thing you eat off it; cf. Fr. *plat*). *Platillo* is a little plate and therefore a 'saucer' (*v.* DOM. APP.).

Platillo also means a 'cymbal' in music (*v.* MUSIC).

plausible. A Falso Amigo: it means 'praiseworthy', 'laudable', i.e. worthy of applause. There is no precise Spanish equivalent of 'plausible' and you will have to do the best you can with *especioso*, 'specious', which, however, is little used.

plumero (m). A feather-duster (v. DOM. APP.).

pollo (m). Chicken (v. FOOD). It applies equally to the live bird.

polvo, hacer. Literally' to make dust', 'to pulverise', but used a great deal metaphorically where we should use some such word as 'shatter'. I quote a few examples:
Las malas noticias le han dejado hecho polvo, 'The bad news has left him shattered'.
Estoy hecho polvo después de tantas juergas, 'I've been on the tiles so much I feel like a wet rag'.
Después de tantos exámenes tengo la vista hecha polvo, 'After all those exams I can hardly see my hand in front of my face'.
Esta carretera hace polvo las cubiertas, 'This road simply ruins the ti res'.

ponerse. This is one of the translations for 'to get'—in the sense of 'become', and the use of it is highly idiomatic and takes a good deal of acquiring, e.g. 'I got nervous', *Me puse nervioso.* It is also, of course, the straightforward word for 'to put on', e.g. *se puso el jersey,* 'he put his cardigan on',[1] but its uses as 'to get' are more numerous and are probably best indicated by a set of examples:
Se puso colorado, 'He blushed', 'He got embarrassed'.
Cuanto más tiempo pasa más fuerte se pone, 'It gets stronger as time goes on' (e.g. tea).
No te pongas tonta, 'Don't be silly', 'Don't get unreasonable'.
¿Quieres ponerte en razón?, 'Don't be absurd', 'Just get this straight' (i.e. 'D'you want to know the right of this?').
Ponerse las botas, 'to make a big profit'.

poner con, 'to put through to' on the telephone. *¿Quiere ponerme con la Señorita. . .?* (v. TELEPHONES).

por eso (v. **eso**).

por lo menos (v. **menos**).

por lo visto (v. **visto**).

portaequipajes (m). Luggage-grid (v. CARS).

postre (m). Literally an 'after', i.e. 'sweet', 'dessert' (v. FOOD).

precioso. In all countries and all periods there are fashionable adjectives for things pleasant and for things unpleasant, e.g. 'Marvellous!' which was recently current in England and still has not died out (*formidable!* also in French) and for things unpleasant—well, 'ghastly' or 'lousy' or what you will. *Precioso* is one of the current Spanish words for things pleasant and therefore equates with 'charming', 'priceless', 'delightful', 'exquisite' (a generation or more ago it would have equated with 'ripping', though there is nothing slangy

---

[1] *Jersey* is essentially something you put your arms into and button up; anything you pull over your head is a *pullover*, though *sweater* also exists.

about *precioso*; it has been in force for a good many years now and may continue for many more). It is not the extreme of high praise, e.g. 'smashing' or 'wizard', which is *estupendo* (*q.v.*). For the extreme of low praise *v.* **asqueroso**.

prevenir. A Falso Amigo since it means not 'to prevent' but 'to warn'. You will need to keep awake about it as in many contexts the difference is not apparent, although real. 'To prevent' is *impedir*.

con prisa. Fast (*v.* MUSIC).

probar. The other word for 'to try', in the sense of 'try out'. 'prove', 'put to the test': *¿Lo has probado?*, 'Have you tried it?'; *Voy a probarlo*, 'I'm going to try it', i.e. to see if it works, if it is all right, if it tastes nice, etc. *Probar* is generally transitive, while *intentar* is intransitive, so that if a noun is to follow immediately *probar* is the word you will almost certainly want; *intentar* is usually followed by a verb or verbal phrase, e.g. *Voy a intentar entrar en la casa*, 'I'm going to try and get into the house', but *Voy a probar la cerradura*, 'I'm going to try the lock'.

profesor. Something of a Falso Amigo as its ordinary meaning is simply 'teacher'. The Spanish for 'Professor' is *Catedrático*. As a title attached to somebody's name it may do service in either language, but you should bear in mind that it brings with it far less prestige in Spanish than in English.

proporcionar, -se. 'To provide with' and 'to provide oneself with', respectively. This is one of those pleasantly imprecise words which permit a somewhat humorous usage as it suggests that the exact means of provision need not be too closely looked into. Whether transitive or reflexive it usually implies that some difficulty is involved in the process. *Proporcionar* might be translated 'to get . . . for', 'to find . . . for' or even 'to sell', especially when the deal is not a legal one (smuggling, black market, etc.); *Juan me proporciona tabaco rubio*, 'John provides me with American cigarettes'; *Mi tío me proporcionó esta colocación*, 'My uncle found me this job'; *Creo que él te puede proporcionar un coche nuevo muy barato*, 'I think he'll be able to sell you a brand-new car at a very low price'.

'To acquire' might be quite a good translation of *proporcionarse*; *Conseguí proporcionarme un mechero*, 'I managed to acquire a cigarette lighter'. The euphemisms used in the Services, such as 'to borrow' and 'to find', which the law would regard as just plain stealing, might conveniently be covered by *proporcionarse*. Such a nuance, however, would be indicated by the context and the tone of voice; *proporcionarse* can be used quite straightforwardly to mean 'to get hold of', 'to obtain', without any suggestion of illegality.

propósito, a. This has two remarkably different meanings, viz. 'incidentally' (cf. Fr. *à propos*) and 'on purpose', but it is not difficult to distinguish between them since the difference depends on whether it comes at the beginning or the end of the sentence. *A propósito, ¿ha visto Lo que el Viento se llevó?*, 'Incidentally, have you seen "Gone With the Wind"? ' but *Lo ha hecho a propósito*, 'He did it on purpose'. *Deliberadamente* also exists and would be possible for 'on purpose' but it has rather the strict sense of 'with deliberation' and *a propósito* sounds much more authentic in conversation.

prospecto (m). A Falso Amigo; it is not a 'prospect' but a 'prospectus', i.e. a brochure setting something out. A 'prospect' would properly be *perspectiva* (or, of course, *panorama*) but the translation will vary according to circumstances, e.g. 'What a prospect!', *¡Qué futuro!*; 'I'm delighted at the prospect of meeting you', *Me encantaría encontrarle*. *Perspectiva* is not a great deal used.

público. You may not need this much but I draw it to your attention as the usual word for 'audience': *El conferenciante dijo al público . . .*, 'The lecturer told the audience . . .'; *¿Había mucho público?*, 'Was there a large audience?' If you mean 'the public' it is usually better to say *el gran público*. An *Audiencia* is what the Pope gives you.

Respetable público, 'Ladies and Gentlemen', and is just as common as, and perhaps even better than, *Señoras y Caballeros*.

pues. 'Well!' i.e. the sort of introduction to a sentence that you say without thinking (cf. Fr. *Eh bien!*) and said unconsciously a hundred times a day. *Pues, tengo que irme*, 'Well, I must go'; *Pues sí*, 'Well, yes'. *Pues entonces*, 'Well, then'; even a long-drawn out 'Well . . . ' is *Pues . . .*, and the final 's' is dragged into a 'z'. It should not take long for you to acquire it.

puesta en marcha (f). Self-starter (*v.* also **arranque**).

pullover (m). Pronounced approximately as in English and as if the 'l' were single but with more emphasis on the last syllable. It means just what it does in English. Also *pulóver*.

punto. A 'point', yes, but here a 'full stop'. **punto y coma,** 'semicolon', and **dos puntos,** 'colon'. **punto y aparte,** 'paragraph', when you are dictating or reading; (*párrafo* is only applied to the completed article, e.g. 'In the third paragraph', *En el tercer párrafo*) (*v.* OFF. APP.).

puntillo, the little dot used in music to increase the value of a note by a half; for the adjective 'dotted' you say *con puntillo* (*v.* MUSIC).

punto muerto (m). Normally this means 'deadlock', e.g. *Las negociaciones de Kaesong llegaron a un punto muerto*, 'The Kaesong negotiations reached deadlock', but in connection with cars (or more precisely, their gears) it means 'neutral': 'I left it in neutral', *Lo dejé en punto muerto* (*v.* CARS).

puré. Mashed; *puré de patata*, 'mashed potatoes' (though in Spain they tend to be rather wetter and sloppier) (*v.* FOOD).

puro (m). Contrary to the usual belief, and many grammar-books, *cigarro* is *not* the Spanish for a 'cigar'; the word is *puro*. *Un puro* is 'a cigar' and do not let anybody try to tell you otherwise. *Cigarro* is used, but to mean 'cigarette', and is about as common as *cigarrillo*, though commoner than either in colloquial speech is *pitillo* (*q.v.*).

Q

qué tal (*v.* tal).

que va (*v.* va, vaya, etc.).

quedar, -se. To stay, to be left, to remain. You know this, I feel sure, and would have little difficulty in saying *Me quedé tres días en Burgos*, 'I stayed three days in Burgos', but when you mean 'Is there any wine left?' would you remember to say simply *¿Queda vino?* and, if somebody asked you for more, to say *No queda* for 'There isn't any more'?

Other uses of *quedar* are more idiomatic, though very common, but can be remembered more easily if you know the Latin origin, which is perhaps rather surprising: it comes from *quietare*, i.e. to quieten, to pacify, to still, and, therefore, to settle. *¿En qué quedamos?*, 'What have we decided?', 'What's our final decision?' and in practice, 'What's it to be?' or 'When's it to be?' From this it is but a short step to such common phrases as *He quedado con Paquita a las seis*, 'I've got an appointment with Paquita (Francisca) at 6 o'clock' (i.e. 'I've settled with Paquita for 6 o'clock'). In other words, the normal translation of *quedar con*, 'to have a date with', 'to agree to meet', 'to have an interview with', and *quedar en*, 'to agree', 'to settle'.

querer. There is little to be said about this verb except to remind you that it means 'to love' as well as 'to want'. *¿Quiere Vd. ayudarme en esto?* is a perfectly normal and polite way of saying, 'Would you like to give me a hand with this?' but *Porque te quiero*, 'Because I love you'.

Querer bien is sometimes used as between people of the same sex to mean approximately 'to like' (cf. Fr. *aimer bien*) though usually when associated with saying something unpleasant or derogatory, e.g. *Te digo esto porque te quiero bien*, 'I mention this to you because I like you'. More usual ways of indicating 'to like', however (and with no unpleasant associations), are *tener afecto a* or *apreciar*: *Le aprecio mucho*, 'I like him very much'.

Quiero is a cliché in cards for 'I'll see you'.

It might be as well to disabuse your mind of the notion that *querido* means 'dear'; it means something nearer 'beloved', or at all events 'well-loved', and has not become conventional in the way that 'dear' has. This is perhaps a good moment to consider the whole problem of formal modes of address in letters:

As you no doubt know, the ordinary, minimum form of address is *Muy Señor mío*, which equates with 'Dear Sir'. It indicates that you do not know the person who will read the letter and have no desire to be other than normally straightforward. It is a purely routine expression.

If you are writing to an individual and wish to seem polite to him, either because of his exalted office or reputation or from a desire to suggest such, then the best form is probably *Distinguido Señor* or, if he is, say, a doctor, then *Distinguido Doctor*. This does not imply that you have met him personally but it does suggest that you know about him and consider him to be above routine.

If you have come to know the person to whom you are writing, either personally or as the result of previous correspondence, then *Apreciado Señor* is likely to be appropriate. It equates with 'Dear Mr. So-and-So', and is cordial without being in any way ingratiating. Interchangeable with it is *Estimado Señor* (*v.* **apreciable**).

Querido does not even enter the picture until you have established a personal friendship and even then the most likely form will be *Querido amigo*.

The attachment of the person's name increases both the personal nature of the communication and the cordiality. *Apreciable Señor Fulano* equates with 'My Dear So-and-So' (using the man's surname) in the course of business and public affairs. Equally *Querido amigo Juan* equates with 'My dear John' and is about as far as a man is likely to go in addressing another. To say *Querido Juan* is almost to say 'Dearest John'. Women, on the other hand, are allowed by convention to be more outspokenly affectionate and so can quite properly call one another *Querida Juana* or even *Querida Juanita*, i.e 'Dearest . . .' or 'My dearest . . .'.

If a man addresses a woman in this way it clearly indicates an acknowledged love affair between them. If a man writes to a woman whom he knows well but does not wish to be thought too affectionate and give her ideas he should say *Apreciable amiga* or at the most *Querida amiga*; these equate with 'Dear . . .' and 'My dear . . .' respectively. Also vice versa, *mutatis mutandis*.

It will be seen that Spaniards are a good deal more formal than we are; in their eyes we are almost recklessly affectionate. Even so *querido* does not really mean 'dear', for which Spanish has no precise equivalent.

queso (m). Cheese (v. FOOD).

¡quieto! Quiet!, Keep still!, Down Fido!, Sh . . .', etc. On the face of it this would seem to be a Buen Amigo, but it is not quite as good as it seems since *quieto* refers to movement rather than noise so that a better equivalent would be 'Don't get excited!', 'Keep calm!' If you were expressly calling for silence as opposed to peace you would say *¡Silencio!*

The full phrase for 'keep still!' is, of course, *¡Estese* (or *estate) quieto!* from *estar quieto*.

quinta (f). A fifth, i.e. the interval (v. MUSIC).

quisquilla (f). Shrimp (v. FOOD). Also the note under **gamba**.

quitar, -se. This, by contrast with *quieto*, is a long way from the English 'quit' (though 'quit' would do for *quitarse* in some contexts, e.g. *se quitó*, 'He pushed off', 'he quitted'), and it is such a common word that it deserves a good deal of attention. The root of the difference is that *quitar* is transitive whereas 'quit' is not.

The basic concept is 'to take away' and it extends from this to 'to take off', 'to remove', 'to get (something) away', 'to deprive', 'to whip away', 'to snatch', 'to pinch' (i.e. steal). *Me han quitado el pasaporte*, 'They've taken away my passport'; *Primero hay que quitar la rueda*, 'You'll have to take the wheel off first'; *Le quitaron el reloj*, 'He had his watch pinched'; *Quitó el balón al delantero centro*, 'He got the ball away from the centre-forward'.

In connection with the last example it should be noted that *quitar a* is used when taking away from a person and *quitar de* when from a thing, e.g. *quitó la tapa de la caja*, 'he took the lid off the box', but *quitar un caramelo a un niño*, 'taking candy from a kid'. As a rough guide out of this labyrinth you can regard the translation of *quitar a* as being 'to take away from' and *quitar de* as 'to take off', 'to remove', but bear in mind that it *is* rough and not infallible.

Quitarse is 'to take oneself off', 'to push off', 'to get out of the way': *¡Quítate!* (or *¡Quítese!*), 'Get out of the way!'; *¡Quítate de esa porquería!*, 'Come away from that muck!' (e.g. mother to child); *Vamos a quitarnos de aquí*, 'Let's get out of here', 'Let's move on to some other place'.

A slightly misleading example is *Se ha quitado el sombrero*, 'He has taken his hat off', misleading because it looks reflexive but strictly is not. It is the same construction as *Me han quitado el pasaporte* mentioned above and means literally 'He has taken the hat off himself' which is the Spanish way of putting it. A literal translation of our way into Spanish would be *Ha quitado su sombrero*, but the Spaniards (like most Latins) prefer to relate the personal pronoun to the act (i.e. the verb) whereas we relate it to the thing (i.e. the noun) (cf. Fr. *Il se lavait les mains*, 'He was washing his hands').

R

radiador (m). Radiator (*v.* CARS).

ranura (f). A slot, e.g. of a telephone. For what you put into it, see **ficha** (*v.* TELEPHONES).

raro. Yes, it does mean 'rare', but chiefly in poetry, etc., and colloquially it bears a similar relation to 'rare' as 'priceless' in English does to 'without price'; and just as 'priceless' in, for example, 'Jesu, priceless treasure', can have a faintly ridiculous sound owing to our modern debasement of the word, so has *raro* become debased in modern Spanish into meaning 'funny' ('funny-peculiar'; 'funny ha-ha' is *gracioso* or *cómico*). *¡Qué raro!*, 'How funny!'; *Pues es una manera muy rara de decirlo*, 'Well, it's a very funny way of putting it'.

  Raro is correct for, e.g., a rare stamp, but you should be careful of the word and confine the use of it to the meaning 'funny'; if you mean 'rare' use *poco frecuente*.

rato (m). A 'while'; *ratito*, 'a little while'. *Salió hace un rato*, 'He went out a while ago'; *Voy a dormir un ratito*, 'I'm going to have a nap'; *Volverá dentro de un ratito*, 'He'll be back in a moment'. 'A long while' would be *un rato largo*, but you might often say *Mucho rato*: 'A long while ago', *Hace mucho rato*, or very often simply *Hace mucho*.

re. D, in MUSIC.

realizar. A rather False Friend, chiefly because in English we mostly confine ourselves to the metaphorical and subjective use of the word whereas in Spanish it is used concretely, i.e. 'to make real' (French does the same). Most often the equation would be 'to take place' (though *tener lugar* is more precise for this), e.g. *El estreno de la ópera se realizó en Madrid*, 'The first performance of the opera took place in Madrid'. In this context the expression 'was performed' would be equally valid, e.g. *La obra se realizó*, 'The work was performed'. 'To happen' or 'to occur' might be other possibilities, but *realizar* suggests a premeditated occurrence which has been long planned rather than something which happens by chance. There is no complete English equivalent and you must simply bear in mind the concept 'to take place' in the sense of 'to bring into reality', 'to bring off', 'to make happen'. *Esperamos realizar este proyecto*, 'We hope to bring off this project' (or '. . . to succeed with'). There are, of course, contexts where 'realise' would be correct, e.g. 'His fondest hopes were realised', *Sus ilusiones más queridas se realizaron*.

realmente. This I mention as it comes as a pleasant surprise, being remarkably parallel to the English 'really'—what one may call a Buen Amigo. *¿Es Vd. realmente inglés?*, 'Are you really English?'; *Pero es realmente un poco tonto,* 'But it is really rather silly'. One place where it would not equate, however, is with 'Really?' said in astonishment; this would be *¿De verdad?,* or more colloquially *¿De veras?,* though you could say *¿Es realmente verdad?* for 'Is that really so?'

In spite of its being a Buen Amigo, however, you will be well advised not to overdo it. *En realidad* is an alternative and perhaps rather commoner.

rebanada (f). Slice (*v.* FOOD).

recado (m). A message, and particularly useful on the telephone. *¿Puede dejar un recado?,* 'Can I give him any message?' (literally 'Can you leave a message?'); *Recibí su recado,* 'I got your message'.

Recadero is, of course, a 'messenger', but it applies to transport agencies and the like. Another word for *recadero* is *ordinario* (*q.v.*). If you wanted to say, 'Can you send me a messenger-boy?' (i.e. to collect something) you would probably say *¿Puede enviar un botones?* (i.e. a 'buttons'), and although this may sound slightly antiquated to us and analogous with 'Where is the bell-pull?' it is by no means so in contemporary Spain. A *botones* is a universal phenomenon; any firm or organisation will have at least one and you need have little compunction in asking them to send him round (*v.* **botones**).

recitativo (m). Recitative (*v.* MUSIC).

recoger. To collect, to pick up, to get; *Van a recogerlo,* 'They're going to call for it'; *¿Hay que ir a recogerlos?,* 'Do we have to go and collect them?' It does not, of course, mean collect in the sense of to make a collection, for which the verb is *coleccionar* (*v.* OFF. APP.).

redoblar. To re-double (*v.* CARDS).

redonda (f). Semibreve (*v.* MUSIC).

refresco (m). Something to refresh yourself with, e.g. a drink. If you mean 'refreshment' in the general sense you must use the plural: *Quiosco de refrescos,* 'refreshment kiosk'.

registro (m). Register, in most contexts, including MUSIC (*q.v.*). It does not, however, mean 'registration' which is *matrícula* (*q.v.*).

regla (f). Ruler, i.e. to make straight lines with (*v.* OFF. APP.).

regular. This is both a verb and an adjective. The verb is straightforward and simply means 'to regulate', e.g. *Regular el tráfico es misión del policía,* 'Regulating traffic is the policeman's job'. I am more concerned, however, with the adjective, which is something of a Falso Amigo. It means 'so-so', 'all right', 'not bad', 'ordinary', 'usual'. Q. *¿Qué tal era?* A. *Regular.* Q. 'What was it like?' A. 'Not bad', 'Fair to middling'. If you are thinking of translating *The Gondoliers* into Spanish do not, I beg you, describe Gilbert's royal queen as *regular*; the translation would have to be *verdadera, genuina, auténtica,* or something of the sort, but I have already warned you of the difficulties of translating Gilbert (*v.* **echar**). *v.* also **corriente,** which is another word for 'ordinary'.

reina (f). Queen, in CARDS (*q.v.*). In Spanish cards she is replaced by a *Caballo* (*q.v.*).

relación (f). By way of being a False Friend since a common use of it is to mean a 'list' (though *lista* is also used); *¿Puede darme la relación de socios?*, 'Can you give me the list of members?'; *Voy a hacer una relación,* 'I'll make a list (of them)'. In many contexts, however, it equates with 'relation': *Tenían relaciones oficiales,* 'They were in official relations with each other'.

The usual Spanish word for a 'relation' in the sense of a 'relative', i.e. a member of one's family, is *familiar* or *pariente*: 'He's broken off relations with all his relations', *Ha roto las relaciones con todos sus familiares* (or *parientes*).

remedio (m). Yes, 'remedy', but brought into Spanish speech fairly often. A cliché worth learning is *No hay más remedio,* 'It can't be helped', 'There's nothing to be done about it', 'There's no two ways about it' (cf. Fr. *tant pis*; Amer. 'It's just too bad').[1] *No tuvo más remedio,* 'He couldn't help it', 'It wasn't his fault'.

remolacha (f). Beets. (*v.* FOOD).

renta (f). 'Rent', quite simply. *Alquiler* (*q.v.*) may also be used in this sense.

repartir. To deal out, to share out, to issue, to dish out. 'To dish out the rations', *Repartir el suministro* (in the Army, for example. *v.* **suministro**). I include it here as it is the proper word for 'to deal' at cards, though *dar* (*las cartas*) is likely to occur more often colloquially.

repente, de. There is nothing colloquial about this and you should know already that it means 'suddenly'. I mention it because you may be tempted to say *súbitamente,* or something of the sort, and although this word exists it is most unlikely that a Spaniard would say it in conversation.

repuesto, de. Spare; *rueda de repuesto,* 'spare wheel' (*v.* CARS).

reserva, de. Another possible translation of 'spare'. Clearly it means 'in reserve' and perhaps a better translation would be 'extra'; *Tengo uno de reserva,* 'I've got one extra' or 'I've got a spare one'. *De repuesto* means more precisely a 'replacement' (*v.* also **sobrar**). The difference between *de reserva* and *de sobra* is that *de reserva* indicates planning whereas *de sobra* indicates chance.

[1] But see also **vamos**.

restar. Another Falso Amigo. It does not mean 'to remain' (as in French), still less 'to rest'. It is transitive in Spanish and means 'to deduct': *Resta el número que habías pensado,* 'Take away the number you first thought of'. (*Deducir* and *sustraer* might also be used but they tend to mean 'to deduce' and 'to steal', respectively.) 'To rest', *Descansar* (*v.* **descanso**).

resultar. 'To result', but in English we use this verb far less than 'to turn out', 'to happen'. *Las fotografías han resultado bien,* 'The photographs have turned out well'; *¿Qué va a resultar de eso?,* 'What will happen about it?'

A common cliché is *resulta que* (or *con el resultado que*), 'with the result that', 'consequently', and in practice probably 'and so' or 'so', in the course of telling a story: '. . . and so her efforts were completely wasted', . . . *resulta que sus esfuerzos fueron completamente vanos.* This cliché is distinctly colloquial.

Where 'so that' means 'in such a manner that' you should use *así que,* e.g. 'Arrange it so that it doesn't fall down', *Arréglelo así que* (or *de manera que*) *no caiga.*

retén (m). Oil-seal (*v.* CARS).

retrete (m). Literally 'retreat' and therefore 'water-closet' (*v.* DOM. APP.).

rey (m). King, at CARDS. He occurs both in Spanish and ordinary packs.

rodaballo (m). Turbot (*v.* FOOD).

rodamiento (**a bolas**) (m). (Ball) bearings (*v.* CARS).

rodillo (m). Roller, e.g. of a typewriter (*v.* OFF. APP.).

rueda (f). Wheel (*v.* CARS). *Rueda de repuesto,* 'Spare wheel'.

ruego, le. From *rogar.* It is very polite, and means 'Will you please . . .', 'I beg you to . . .', etc. (Fr. *'Je vous prie de . . .'*).[1] *Le ruego acepte estas flores,* 'I trust you will accept these flowers' (and you may care to know that it is *de rigueur* in Spain to send flowers to one's hostess on the day after being invited to dine at her house—or at any rate, at the end of one's stay).

S

sábana (f). A sheet for a bed (*v.* DOM. APP.).

saber, ¿sabe? *¿Sabe?* is perhaps hardly worth mentioning but it equates so closely with the English 'You know' that it might almost be called a Buen Amigo: *Tiene casi cuarenta años, ¿sabe?,* 'He's nearly forty, you know' (and if the answer is

[1] If you want the French *'Je vous en prie'*, without anything to follow, then the usual Spanish would be *No faltaría más* (q.v.) or *Por Dios* (q.v.), or both together.

'Yes, I know' the Spanish is not *Sí, sé*, it is *Sí, ya lo sé* (*v.* **ya**)). It is the origin of the word 'savvy'.

A cliché derived from *saber* which you may care to learn is *Y no sé qué y no sé cuánto* (or *y no sé qué más*), which means 'and so on and so forth' or 'and what not', 'I don't know what all', etc.

¿Qué sé yo? is another cliché and means 'What do *I* know?', 'How should *I* know?', 'I wouldn't know', or even 'One never knows'; e.g. *Me dijo que vendría pero ¿qué sé yo?*, 'He said he would come but one never knows'.

Yet another cliché is *¡Tú que sabes!* a crushing remark which is usually made in a sarcastic tone of voice and equates with 'How do *you* know!', 'What do *you* know about it!', 'Wise   guy!', etc. As in the English equivalents, it is a legacy from childhood, hence the 2nd person singular. It is unlikely to be said in the 'polite' form.

sacar. A tremendously common verb which demands a good deal of attention. The best concept is probably 'to extract' but, as so often, you must cast your net wide; *extraer* exists for the precise equivalent of 'extract' and *sacar* is imprecise. It means 'to pull out', 'to take out', 'to get out' (trans.): *Voy a sacar el coche* (*del garaje*), 'I'm going to get the car out (of the garage), *¿Puedes sacar este corcho?*, 'Can you pull this cork out?';[1] *Pues, muy bien, sácalo*, 'All right, then, fish it out'; *Sacó un pitillo*, 'He took out a cigarette'.

Slightly more metaphorical and idiomatic uses of it are:

Me gustaría sacar a Lolita a bailar, 'I should like to have a dance with Dolores' (and not 'take Dolores to a dance', which would be *llevar a bailar*).

Sacó buenas notas en sus exámenes, 'He got high marks in his exams'.

Sacar also means 'to serve' at tennis or table-tennis and 'to kick off' at football.

Sonsacar is a rather special verb meaning 'to pump', in the metaphorical sense, i.e. 'to elicit information', 'to make talk'.

sal (f). Salt (*v.* FOOD).

salchicha (f). Sausage. **salchichón** (m), a sort of salami sausage, a mosaic of meats, and often pretty tough (*v.* FOOD).

salir. As you know very well, it means 'to go out', 'to come out', 'to emerge', but it extends to many metaphorical uses and therefore often equates with 'to turn out', 'to work', e.g. *A lo mejor no me sale*, 'It probably won't work', 'I probably shan't manage it'; *Ha salido bien*, 'It's come out nicely' (e.g. of a photograph).

The translation would quite often be 'get' in the sense of 'become' and I recommend a mental note to this effect as there is no current word for 'become' in Spanish.[2] An indication

---

[1] *Sacacorchos* (m), Corkscrew.
[2] For other translations of 'become', *v.* **hacerse, pasar, volverse, ponerse.**

that the lack of word is felt may be seen from the fact that some writers, notably doctors and research workers, use the word *devenir*, whose French origin is obvious. This use of it, however, is practically confined to works of a scientific nature and although such use may well extend and become general in the future you should be aware that it is far from colloquial at the moment.

salmón (m). Salmon. **salmonete** (m). Red mullet (*v.* FOOD).

salsa (f). Sauce (*v.* FOOD).

sano. A Falso Amigo. It denotes physical health only and has no connection whatever with mental. 'Sane', *cuerdo*.

sardina (f). Sardine (*v.* FOOD). In Spain they are often eaten fresh and are delicious.

sartén (f). Frying-pan (*v.* DOM. APP.). The most popular Spanish cooking utensil.

saxofón (m). Saxophone (*v.* MUSIC).

sea (o). This is not a very important expression but Spaniards use it a remarkable amount and it usually introduces an alternative way of saying something just said, so that the equivalents are 'that's to say' (Fr. *c'est à dire*), 'in other words', 'in short'. Quite often we should say 'I mean' and just as many English people may scatter 'I mean' rather liberally about their conversation when in fact they mean nothing except that they are feeling shy or nervous, e.g. when trying to explain something difficult, so do some Spaniards tend to scatter *o sea*.

secante (m). Blotting paper; it is short for *papel secante*, i.e. drying paper (*v.* OFF. APP.).

segmento (m). Piston-ring (*v.* CARS).

seguir. 'To follow', of course, also 'to continue', hence 'to go on': 'To go on drinking', *Seguir bebiendo*; 'The barber went on shaving', *El barbero siguió afeitando*, or just plain 'Go on!', *¡Sigue!*; 'Carry on! carry on!', *¡Sigue, sigue!* It means 'follow' when a noun follows it, e.g. *Seguía las vías del tranvía*, 'He was following the tram-lines'.

según. 'According to', 'as', and very common. *Pues, según*, 'Well, it's all according'; 'It all depends'. *A mi parecer*, 'In my opinion' or '*I* think', with an accent on the *I*; *Según Pablo hay nueve*, 'Pablo says there are nine'. It is not merely colloquial; in a serious, scholarly work you might see *Según vamos a ver en el próximo capítulo*, 'As we shall see in the next chapter', and the four gospels are entitled *El Evangelio según* . . . (*S. Mateo, S. Marcos, S. Lucas y S. Juan*).

A more colloquial phrase for '*I* think' is *Digo yo* (*v.* **diga**).

seguro, seguramente. *Seguro* means 'safe' and 'certain' right
enough but it also means 'certainly'. You might be tempted
to think that this is mere slackness and that *seguramente* would
be the full version, but in fact *seguro*, when used to mean
'certainly', is short for *Está seguro*, or *Es seguro*, 'It's certain',
'There's no doubt'. *Seguramente*, on the other hand, means
simply 'no doubt' and just as in English 'no doubt' immediately suggests that there is doubt so does *seguramente* in
Spanish. Let us therefore get it quite straight:
> *Seguro*, 'certainly', 'there's no doubt about it' (i.e. denotes
> certainty).
> *Seguramente*, 'probably', 'no doubt' (i.e. denotes un-
> certainty).

semicorchea (f). Semiquaver. **semifusa** (f). Demi-demi-
semiquaver. **semitono** (m). Semitone (*v.* MUSIC).

señas (f). 'Name and address', 'particulars', but as often as not
just 'address'. In our grammars we learn *dirección* which is
perfectly correct but less often used. *¿Puede darme sus señas?*,
'Can you give me your (his) address?' If, however, you know
neither the name nor the address of the person and said
¿Puede darme las señas del Director del Conservatorio? it would
suggest that you wanted his name as well.
> *Señas* also means 'features': *Sus señas principales son . . .*,
> 'Its main features are . . .'.
> 'Special peculiarities', *Señas particulares*, e.g. on an
identity card.

sensible. A False Friend, since it means 'sensitive'. It does not
even equate with the special use of 'sensible' in such examples
as 'I am very sensible of the honour you do me'. 'Sensible'
would be *sensato* or *práctico*. Also, there is the noun:

sensible (m). Leading-note (*v.* MUSIC).

sesos (m. pl.). Brains.

si. B, in Music. Bach's B minor Mass is often loosely referred to
as the *Misa en Si* (*v.* MUSIC).

sí, sí-. With the accent on the first *sí* and said in a sing-song, sarcastic tone of voice has the effect of discounting what has just
been said and is the equivalent of 'I don't think', or perhaps
more exactly the American 'O yeah!' It indicates fairly
frankly that you do not believe a word of what you have just
been told.

¡sí señor! This is simply an emphatic way of saying 'Yes',
especially when contradicting, and therefore equates with
'Oh yes it is!', 'Yes, indeed!', 'Yes, sir!', 'Yes, sirree!' (Fr.
si!). It is a cliché and consequently is used to a woman in
this same form (i.e. is not converted into *Sí señora*).

siempre. 'Always', of course, but a convenient and very common way of handling the word 'usual'; *como siempre*, 'as usual'; *lo de siempre*, 'the usual' or 'the usual thing'; *del modo de siempre*, 'in the same old way'.

silencio (m). Silence, but in music a rest (not a pause) (*v.* MUSIC).

silla (f), **-ón** (m). A *silla*, 'chair'; *sillón* 'arm-chair' (*v.* also **butaca**) (*v.* DOM. APP.).

simpático. Rather a classic Falso Amigo. In Spanish (and most other European languages (Fr. *sympathique*, Ger. *sympathisch*, Ital. *simpatico*, etc.) the meaning is 'nice' as applied to a person, i.e. of attractive personality, easy to get on with, etc.: *Es un chico muy simpático*, 'He's an awfully nice chap'. English seems to be the only European language which has the connotation of compassionate, condoling, etc., although this meaning is rather suggested by the original Greek συν= with, παθος=suffering. The Spanish for 'sympathetic' is *compasivo*.

simple. An Unreliable Friend: applied to things it means 'simple', as in English, but of people it means 'simple-minded' and, as in English, is something of a euphemism for 'stupid'. 'A simple person' would be *una persona sencilla*.

sin triunfos. No trumps (*v.* CARDS).

si no, sino. *Si no* means 'if not' or 'unless', but it is more difficult to remember that *sino* means 'but' (i.e. 'so much as'). 'If it is not raining . . .', *Si no llueve . . .*; 'It wasn't the wine but the food', *No fué el vino sino la comida*; Pope Gregory's famous alleged remark: 'Not Angles but angels' would be *No anglos sino ángeles* in modern Spanish. You have to get the ideograph 'Not . . . but . . .' into your head and then equate it with *No . . . sino. . . . El Sino* means 'Fate'.

sobrar, tener de sobra. A curious verb meaning 'to be left over', 'to remain', 'to be surplus'. You should be clear as to the distinction with *quedar*, which also means 'to remain'; if you say *¿Queda vino?* it means 'Is there any wine left?' but suggests that you are still sitting at the table and could do with some more; if you say *¿Sobra vino?* it means 'Is there any wine left over?' and suggests a hostess surveying the scene when the meal is over and the guests have gone. It is the sort of verb which it is very difficult to use in time though the most illiterate Spaniard will use it a dozen times a day. I quote a few examples:

Después de repartir las cartas sobraba una, 'After dealing the cards there was one left over'.

Aunque estoy de vacaciones no me sobra tiempo, 'Although I'm on holiday I don't seem to have any spare time'.

Tenemos tiempo de sobra, 'We've got plenty of time'.

De sobra is a convenient phrase for 'extra': *Tengo uno de sobra*, 'I've got one extra' (*v.* also **reserva**).

sobre (m). Envelope (*v.* OFF. APP.).

sofá (m). Sofa, as in English (*v.* DOM. APP.). Very easy, but note the gender.

sol. G (not the dominant) (*v.* MUSIC).

soler. A difficult verb to remember to use as there is no exact equivalent in English, though it is very common. It means 'to be wont to', 'to be in the habit of', 'to always . . .':[1] *Suele pasear por las noches*, 'He's in the habit of going for walks at night'; *Suelen salir alrededor de las siete*, 'They always come out about 7 o'clock'.

It is the proper translation for the habitual present tense: e.g. 'I smoke twenty cigarettes a day', *Suelo fumar veinte cigarros al día*; 'I see him on Fridays', *Le suelo ver los viernes*. A careful mental note is indicated and some practice recommended.

solo, -ista. In music the meanings are as in English, i.e. *solo*, 'solo', and *solista*, 'soloist', though gender will vary according to circumstances. The expression *solistas*, however, in an orchestral context, is likely to mean 'single desks'.

solomillo (m). Beef-steak; sirloin (*v.* FOOD).

soltar. A difficult verb; it means 'to leave alone', 'to let go of', 'to get clear of', 'to release'. *Suéltelo*, 'Let go of it'; *¡Suélteme, canalla!*, 'Unhand me, villain!' It is the opposite of *coger*.

sonar. To sound, but a common expression is *Eso me suena*, 'That reminds me (of something)', 'That strikes a chord'. If you were reading the newspaper and the news was gloomy you might say *Esto me suena a guerra*, 'It looks like war to me'.

Sonar also means 'to ring' of a telephone (but not 'ring up', which is *llamar*), e.g. *el teléfono está sonando*, 'the telephone's ringing'. 'To ring the bell', however, is *tocar el timbre*.

sopa (f). Thick soup (*v.* FOOD).

sostén (m). Brassière.

sostenido (m). 'Sustained' in most contexts, including music, if it means '*sostenuto*'; in music, however, it has the additional meaning of 'sharp' (♯); *Sol sostenido*, 'G sharp' (*v.* MUSIC).

sota (f). Literally 'page boy'; in cards we call him Knave or Jack. He occurs in both Spanish and ordinary packs and his gender is feminine (*v.* CARDS).

soy yo. The literal translation of this sounds absurd since what could be more obvious than the fact that 'I am I'? Perhaps, if Moses had been a Spaniard, Jehovah might have uttered the words from the burning bush. Certainly Louis XIV would have needed them before a Spanish *Parlement* when saying

---

[1] I make no apology for the implied split infinitive.

'*L'état, c'est moi*', for which the Spanish would be *El estado soy yo*.[1] Our somewhat regrettable contemporary equivalent is 'That's me!' though it might be 'Here!' or 'Present!' or just 'Yes!' according to circumstance. You may need it more than you think: at Spanish frontier posts it is often customary to collect all passports and disappear with them into an office and when the formalities within have been completed a gentleman emerges with them and proceeds to call out the names. When your name comes the correct response is *¡Soy yo!* whereupon you go up and get it, and it is a nice point whether you will have more difficulty in recognising your name when you hear it than in remembering to say *¡Soy yo!* when you do recognise it. *Soy yo* is also a normal response on the telephone when someone asks for you and you yourself are replying, though an alternative for this is *¡al habla!* (i.e. 'speaking!') When you are calling, on the telephone, also you do not say '*It's* Antonio (speaking)', i.e. *Es Antonio*, you say *Soy Antonio*, i.e., 'I am Antonio', which is quite logical.

st . . . st . . . st . . . This is an attempt to indicate the clicking noise made between the tongue and the upper teeth. In English it indicates shocked surprise of a mild form; in Spanish it merely indicates the negative and is equivalent to 'Good gracious, no!', 'What an absurd idea!' or just a desultory 'No' or 'No, no, my boy!'

suave. Soft, and the usual word for it in music: *Más suave*, 'Quieter', 'Softer' (*v.* MUSIC).

subasta (f). The 'bidding'. **subastar.** 'To bid' in certain Spanish card games of the poker type. In bridge you do not use *subastar* but *marcar* (*v.* CARDS).

subdominante (f). Subdominant (*v.* MUSIC).

subir. You should know this, but it may be worth while reminding you that it means 'to go up' and *not* 'to undergo', as its etymology or a knowledge of French might lead you to suppose: *Los precios han subido*, 'Prices have gone up'; *Tenemos que subir por la escalera*, 'We shall have to walk up' (the lift being, as usual, out of order).

suburbio (m). This Amigo is Falso in its associations rather than in its literal meaning. It does in fact mean the regions on the outskirts of a city, but in Spain such quarters are mostly very poor and if you tell a Spaniard *Vivo en los suburbios de Londres*, he will imagine you live in a slum. Of recent years a few high-class suburbs have been built but these receive a special name, e.g. *Colonia de 'El Viso'* on the outskirts of Madrid, and are certainly not referred to as *suburbios* though they may be as

[1] Italian uses the same idiom, cf. the famous remark of Pope Pius IX when Cardinal Guidi pointed out to him that Papal Infallibility was not in accordance with Catholic tradition: '*La tradizione son io.*' An English pope would have had to say '*I* am tradition' with an accent on the 'I' since it is not to be supposed he would have said anything so crude as 'Tradition! that's me!'

afueras. Incidentally, the villas in such high-class suburbs are often referred to as *hoteles*, although, unlike the usual Spanish practice, they are wholly occupied by one family.

suizo (m). A kind of roll, superficially like those Swiss breakfast rolls that are cloven down the middle. They are normally served for breakfast in Spanish hotels.

suministro (m). Rations, supplies. This is quite a proper word and not necessarily colloquial, but in this unfortunate contemporary world it all too often occurs in ordinary domestic conversation.

superdominante (f). Superdominant. **supertónica** (f). Supertonic (*v*. MUSIC).

susto (m). A 'turn', a 'fright', a 'shock': 'You did give me a turn!', *¡Qué susto me has dado! Dar* is used to 'give' a shock but when it is a matter of receiving one you say *llevarse*, e.g. *Vaya susto que se llevó mi madre cuando no volví a casa*, 'What a scare my mother got when I didn't come home'.

Asustar, 'to shock', 'to frighten' may also be used instead of *dar un susto* but it is less common colloquially, though *asustado* is quite common for 'frightened', 'scared'.

T

tal, qué tal. 'So' or 'such'. *El Señor Tal*, 'Mr. So-and-So'; *Tal señor*, 'Such a man' or 'Any such man' (though *El tal señor* would be a rather derogatory way of saying 'That chap'); *Tal, tal y tal* (usually accompanied by a gesture), 'Whatever it may be', 'And so on and so on', i.e. when hopping quickly over unimportant details (though *etcétera, etcétera* can also be used).

¿Qué tal? is the almost universal greeting between people who have met before and are on comparatively equal terms, and the shade of familiarity is indicated by other words in connection with it, thus *¡Hola! ¿qué tal?* is fairly familiar and would be used between colleagues in the same office or people of equal status who knew each other well; *¿Qué tal está Vd.?* is more polite, though it is cordial, and it really is a question so that it requires some such answer as *Muy bien, gracias ¿y Vd.?* *¿Qué tal?* by itself barely requires an answer (like the English 'What cheer?') and can be replied to merely by another *¿Qué tal?* If you wanted a reply at the familiar level you would say *¿Qué tal te va?*, or something of the sort, i.e. 'How are you getting on?' *¿Qué tal está Vd.?* is something like 'How are you?'

It is important to distinguish between *ser* and *estar* when using *¿qué tal?* *¿Qué tal es?* means 'What's it (or he or she) like?' whereas *¿Qué tal está?* means 'How is it (or he or she)?', i.e. 'What state is it (he, she) in'. Foreigners of all sorts, as we know, are continually saying in English, 'How is it?' when they mean 'What is it like?' but Spaniards, if they have learned their English carefully, should not be in danger of making the mistake. Few things could demonstrate better the essential difference between *ser* and *estar*.

Qué tal si . . . is a useful phrase for 'How about . . .' or 'Suppose'.

taladrar, taladro. Punch, i.e. for perforating paper.

Taladro is the apparatus and *taladrar* is the verb for using it (*v.* OFF. APP.).

tampoco. As you must be aware, it means 'neither', 'not either', 'nor', and there are many occasions where we should say simply 'No'. 'He hasn't come either', *El no ha venido tampoco*; 'Neither do I', *Yo tampoco*. Q. 'Did you get the beans?' A. 'No, I forgot those too'. Q. *¿Has cogido las judías?* A. *Tampoco*, simply. Negative replies to a series of questions on the same subject are all *Tampoco* after the initial 'No', thus: Q. 'Were the López's there?' A. 'No'. Q. 'The García's?' A. 'No'. Q. 'The Romero-Sánchez's?' A. 'No, they weren't there either'. Q. *¿Estaban los López?* A. No. Q. *¿Los García?* A. *Tampoco*. Q. *¿Los Romero-Sánchez?* A. *Tampoco* (or *ellos tampoco*). The basic concept (and the literal meaning) is 'equally little' and you must remember to use it the moment there is something to be equally little to.

tanto, -s. How would you refer to the 1920's in Spanish? The answer is *los veintitantos*.[1] 'In the 'thirties', *en los treinta y tantos*; *Ha durado unos cincuenta y tantos años*, 'It's been going on for fifty-odd years'.

Un tanto is a counter used in card games of the poker type. Five of them make a *marreco* (*q.v.*).

tapa, tapadera (f). Lid (*v.* DOM. APP.). Either form may be used indiscriminately.

Tapacubos, 'hub cover' (*v.* CARS).

tapas (f). A more current and colloquial word for *aperitivos*, in the Spanish sense, i.e. 'snacks', little things to eat with your drinks, e.g. salted almonds, olives, prawns, *calamares*, *boquerones*, and a multitude of other delicacies. In many cafés you will be given something automatically, but occasionally you may be asked *¿Quiere tapas?*, in which case you specify what you would like.

The word *tapas* is commoner in Andalusia than anywhere else in Spain. It is therefore more likely to be heard in *tabernas* or restaurants with *ambiente andaluz* than in fashionable cafés, where the word *aperitivos* is always preferred.

tapón (m). Plug of a basin (*v.* DOM. APP.).

taquígrafo, -a. Shorthand-typist; **taquigrafía,** shorthand (*v.* OFF. APP.).

[1] *Veinte* is the only number which contracts in this way.

taquilla (f). A 'guichet', a window, of the ticket-office sort, and found in banks, post-offices, etc. The 'box-office' in the metaphorical sense, i.e. the takings at a theatre, is referred to as the *taquilla* (and of course in the literal sense as well).

tarde (f). Sometimes this has to be translated 'evening' and some-times 'afternoon', and the only way to get the feeling of it is to understand how Spaniards unconsciously divide up their day in their own minds. *Mañana* is 'morning' and in both coun-tries it is the period between getting up and having lunch. During this period you say *Buenos días*. *Buenas tardes* covers the period between lunch and dinner but it is complicated slightly by the fact that *noche* means predominantly 'dark', so that in summer, if you dine by daylight it could still be *tarde* after dinner.[1] Eight o'clock in the evening is a time which may be referred to as either *tarde*, if it is still light, or *noche*, if it is dark by that time. What is indubitably *noche* is from 11 o'clock onwards and it should be borne in mind that you can greet a person with *Buenas noches* (it is often rather discon-certing to meet a Spaniard, who imagines he speaks English, arriving at a late party and greeting you with 'Good night!'). Eleven o'clock is by no means late by Spanish standards and the period from 11 p.m. to 2 a.m. is a section of the 24 hours which needs a name to itself.[2]

No doubt our English subdivision of *tarde* into 'afternoon' and 'evening' is due to the existence of tea as a meal time.

tarta (f). Tart (*v.* FOOD).

tasca (f). This is very similar in meaning to *taberna* and may therefore be translated 'tavern'. Basically the difference between them is that a *tasca* is primarily for food and a *taberna* for drink, but in practice the difference has come to be of little importance. The word is distinctly colloquial but has become extremely common of recent years. It suggested a place where the food was good and cheap but served without refinements such as complicated cutlery, and where you could eat a *chuleta* using your fingers, and consequently it attracted the *nouveaux riches* brought to the surface by the present régime. By now it has become an everyday word and *comer* (*cenar*) *en plan de tasca* almost a cliché.

taza (f), **-ón** (m). *Taza*, 'cup'; *tazón*, 'big cup' and, therefore, 'bowl' (*v.* DOM. APP.).

té (m). Tea (*v.* FOOD). It is little drunk in Spain and is usually abominably weak. It will probably take you a long time to get your *chica* to make it properly.

---

[1] Perhaps rather an unlikely contingency in Madrid and the south as people dine so late.
[2] The 'first' and 'second' houses at Spanish cinemas and theatres are at 7 p.m. (approximately) and 11 p.m. (approximately) respectively and here the distinction between *tarde* and *noche* is clear: *¿Vas por la tarde o por la noche?* is 'Are you going to the first or second house?' even in winter, when it is dark for both your houses.

tecla (f.). Key of a piano or organ (*v.* MUSIC); also of a typewriter (*v.* OFF. APP.).

tenazas (f. pl.). Pincers (*v.* DOM. APP.).

tener que. This is by far the commonest way of indicating 'must'' 'got to', 'have to', especially when attached to a person (the general sense—'it is necessary' (Fr. *il faut*) can be rendered by *hay que, q.v.*). *Tengo que marcharme*, 'I've got to go', 'It's time I went' (or alternatively, *Me tengo que ir*); *Tiene que cuidarse*, 'He'd better be careful'; *Tendrán que llegar a las ocho*, 'They'll have to get there at eight o'clock'. To cement it into your minds let me tell you a story: A young lady was seen on a Spanish beach wearing a two-piece bathing costume, a practice forbidden under the present régime in Spain. A *guardia* came up to her and said *Perdone, señorita, pero los trajes de dos piezas no se permiten; hay que traer trajes de una pieza*, to which the young lady replied *¿Pues, qué pieza me tengo que quitar?*[1]

Tener la banca, in connection with playing cards, means 'to be banker' (*v.* CARDS).

tenor (m.). Tenor (*v.* MUSIC).

tercera (f.). A third, i.e. the interval (*v.* MUSIC).

ternera (f.). Veal (*v.* FOOD). It is probably the commonest of all Spanish meat dishes.

tetera (f.). Strictly speaking a tea-pot, but tea is little drunk in Spain and consequently Spaniards have none of the reverence due to that sacred beverage and tend to use the word *tetera* for a 'kettle', which is likewise unknown. I imported a kettle into Spain but had to give the strictest instructions that nothing but water must ever be cooked in it, otherwise it would have been used for soup, coffee, or what you will, whilst still retaining the name of *tetera* (*v.* DOM. APP.) (*v.* also note under **olla**).

tiempo (m.). Time, but in music it can have a number of different special meanings, viz.:

(*a*) beat; i.e. of a bar: *el tercer tiempo del compás*, 'the third beat of the bar';

(*b*) tempo, i.e. the absolute speed at which a piece is taken;

(*c*) movement, i.e. of a work in several movements: *Lo que más me gusta es el segundo tiempo*, 'It's the second movement I like best'.

tienda (f.). A shop, but unless you specify which kind of shop, e.g. *lechería, carnicería, estanco*, etc., it means a 'general store' or 'grocer's shop'. If you have read the entry under *luego* you will have noticed that she went first to *la tienda*, i.e. 'the grocer's'. The grocer, however, does not put *la tienda* on

---

[1] 'You know, Miss, two-piece bathing-suits aren't allowed, only one-piece,' and the reply, 'Well, which piece do I take off?'

the sign outside his shop, he usually puts *ultramarinos* (*q.v.*) or *tienda de ultramarinos*.

It is also a 'tent' when camping; no doubt the connection is with the somewhat Arabian booths and tabernacles which formed the shopping centres of the past.

tijeras (t. pl.). Scissors (*v.* DOM. APP., OFF. APP.).

timbal (m). Kettledrum, 'timps' (*v.* MUSIC).

tinto. This word originally comes from *teñir*, 'to dye', and literally means 'dyed'. Apart from one or two survivals, however, e.g. *Riotinto*, it is only applied to wine, when it means 'red'. You cannot speak of *el vino rojo* (*v.* FOOD).

tío (m). Literally 'uncle' but used colloquially to mean 'chap', 'bloke', 'fellow'. It has a slightly deprecatory sound so you would not use it if you were being complimentary: *¿Qué tal es el tío ese?*, 'What's he like, that chap?'; *Es un tío bastante raro*, 'He's a funny sort of bloke'.

You must avoid the feminine form, however, and not refer to any woman, of whatever age, as *una tía*, unless she is strictly an aunt, since otherwise it denotes a whore.

tiple (f). Another word for soprano and similar to our treble (*v.* MUSIC). Boys and eunuchs are referred to as having *voces atipladas*.

tirantes (m. pl.). What the English call braces and the Americans suspenders.

tirar. To draw, to pull, but it has several other meanings, e.g. to throw away; it is the usual word for this in domestic circumstances: *¿Hay que tirarlo?*, 'Shall we throw it away?'; *Tíralo*, 'Chuck it away'.

It also means 'To discharge a fire-arm', 'To manage as best one can', 'To fend for oneself', e.g. Gilbert's 'To long for whirlwinds and to have to do the best you can with the bellows', *Desear torbellinos y tener que tirar con el fuelle*. In this sense it is extremely colloquial. Q. *¿Qué tal estás?* A. *Voy tirando.* Q. 'How are you getting on?' A. 'So-so', 'Getting along all right', 'Mustn't grumble', 'Managing somehow', etc. *Puedo tirar*, 'I can just manage'.

Another colloquial meaning is 'to take' in the metaphorical sense, e.g. 'Take the second turning to the right', *Tire por la segunda bocacalle a la derecha* (note the *por*); *Me tiré tres horas haciéndolo*, 'It took me three hours to do it', 'I spent three hours doing it'. Note that in the latter case it becomes reflexive: *tirarse*, 'to spend' (in the metaphorical sense).

tocar. To touch, but also to play a musical instrument (not *jugar* which applies to games, cards, etc.). *¿Toca Vd. el piano?*, 'Do you play the piano?' For these purposes a gramophone counts as a musical instrument and *Está tocando unos discos*, 'He's playing some records'. 'To ring the bell', *tocar el timbre*.

It is used impersonally with *a* to indicate whose turn it is:
Me toca a mí, 'It's my turn'; *Te toca a tí*,   'It's your turn';
Os toca a vosotros, 'It's the turn of you all'; *Le tocaba a Vd.*,
'It was your turn'.

It may also be used in the slang sense of 'to touch', i.e. to
get money: *Me tocó mucho dinero a la lotería*, 'I raked in quite
a bit in the sweepstake'.

tomate (m). Tomato (*v.* FOOD).

tonalidad (f). Key in MUSIC (*q.v.*).

tónica (f). Tonic in music, i.e. the keynote (*v.* MUSIC). 'Tonic' in
the other sense, i.e. something that invigorates, is *tónico*
(masculine).

tono (m). Tone, in music and applying in all senses of the word,
including two semitones (*v.* MUSIC). Also dialling tone (*v.*
TELEPHONES).

tornillo (m). Screw or bolt (*v.* CARS). 'To screw', *atornillar*;
'unscrew', *destornillar*. **destornillador**, 'screwdriver' (*v.*
DOM. APP.).

tortilla (f). Omelette (*v.* FOOD). This is one of the commonest
ways of having your egg course and usually you can choose
the ham, mushroom, French, etc., varieties but they are
seldom as well cooked as in France and all too often olive-oil
is used instead of butter.

trabajo (m). Work, but also 'job' or 'job of work'; you can speak
of *un trabajo*, and when you mean 'an awful job' it is exactly
what you would say: *¡Qué trabajo!*, 'What a job!', 'What an
awful job!'; *Era un trabajo horrible*, 'It was a frightful job';
Me costó mucho trabajo conseguir billetes, 'I had an awful
time   getting tickets'.

traducir. A Falso Amigo though perhaps unlikely to lead you
astray since you will have learnt that it means 'translate' in
the first days of studying Spanish. 'To traduce' would be
translated *calumniar* or *difamar*.

traje (m). A 'suit' of clothes. 'Costume' is also a translation, e.g.
traje de baño, 'bathing costume'. *Traje de etiqueta*, 'evening-
dress' (i.e. white tie and tails).

trampa (f). This is very near slang; it means 'racket', 'wangle',
'fiddle'. The Spaniards have a saying: *Hecha la ley, hecha la
trampa*, which might be translated 'There's your law and there's
your racket', i.e. no sooner is any given law passed than someone will discover a means of making money by circumventing
it.

transmisión (f). Transmission (*v.* CARS).

tranvía. Although literally it should mean a 'tramway', in fact
means a 'tram', i.e. the actual vehicle, not the permanent way

it runs on. 'I caught a tram' is *Cogí un tranvía* and there is *no* word *tran* or *tram*.

trapo (m). A general name for a bit of cloth used about the house and, therefore, a dishcloth, a duster, etc. (floorcloth is more strictly *bayeta* (*q.v.*) being made of rather heavier cloth). A yellow duster has a special name, viz. *gamuza* (*q.v.*), and there is a special kind of duster for flapping around ornaments called *los zorros* (*q.* also *v.*), but unless you are particularly specifying one of these use *trapo*: 'Fetch a cloth', *Traiga un trapo* (*v.* DOM. APP.).

trasladar. The 'n' has slipped out in Spanish but you will no doubt be aware that it does not mean 'translate', not even in the sense that Bottom was translated; it means 'transfer', e.g. *Me han trasladado al departamento extranjero*, 'I've been transferred to the foreign department'. *Transferir* is used for more abstract transfers, e.g. in banking, accountancy, etc. 'To translate', as you know, is *traducir*.

trastorno (m). Not strictly a colloquial word but it occurs often in familiar speech. It means 'disturbance', 'fuss', 'how-d'ye-do'.

trébol (m). A corruption of trifolium (trefoil) (Fr. *trèfle*), i.e. Clubs (*v.* CARDS).

tresillo (m). A triplet (*v.* MUSIC). Not, however, triplets (i.e. three babies at a go), which is *tres hermanos gemelos*.

trino (m). Trill (*v.* MUSIC).

triunfo (m). Triumph, but in card games 'trump' (*v.* CARDS). Triumph is the origin of the English word.

trombón (m). Trombone (*v.* MUSIC).

trompa (f). French horn (*v.* MUSIC).

trompeta (f). Trumpet (*v.* MUSIC).

trucha (f). Trout (*v.* FOOD).

tuba (f). Tuba (*v.* MUSIC).

tubería (f). As the name suggests this is a general word for tubes or pipes about the house and therefore may often mean 'drains', but it cannot be applied to drains of the municipal sort which are of a higher order and called *alcantarillas* (*q.v.*).

tuerca (f). Nut, i.e. counterpart of bolt (*v.* CARS).

tuétano (m). Marrow, i.e. of bones; the vegetable is *calabacín* (*v.* FOOD).

turron (m). An extraordinarily nice Spanish sweetmeat made of almonds and honey. There are many varieties but the two main types are: *Alicante*, in which the nuts are left whole, and *Jijona*, in which they are ground so that it has the consistency of fudge. It is customary to eat it round about Christmas and the New Year.

U

ultramarinos. This is a Friend of such Falsity that there is probably little danger of your being deceived by it, so remarkable is the divergence between the two languages. The basic concept, as the merest smattering of classical education will tell you, is 'beyond the sea', but whereas in English this is applied simply to a colour of blue which surpasses that of the sea, in Spanish it applies to things imported from beyond the sea, more specially to things to eat, and consequently is likely to be the sign above all self-respecting grocers' shops. Not, of course, that much Spanish food is in fact imported, but it gives a nice, exciting, exotic impression to suggest that it has been, just as 'Delicatessen' has an attractive sound in English. *Ultramarinos*, however, is vastly more common than 'Delicatessen', in fact it is usual, though the shop which has the sign is normally referred to as a *tienda* (*q.v.*). The complete name is, of course, *tienda de ultramarinos*.

uva (f). Grape. Normally used in the plural, as in English. It is a common *postre* from about August to December.

V

qué va, vamos, vámonos, vaya. It would perhaps have been more consistent to have put these under **ir,** but as they all begin with **va-** and are all clichés, I think here is better.

¡Qué va! is what you say when you dismiss something with a wave of the hand and it equates with 'I won't hear of it!', 'Good heavens, no!', 'Of course not', 'Nonsense', 'Not a bit of it', 'Don't believe a word of it', according to circumstances and tone of voice. If someone says, 'Now you must let me pay for my share of the dinner', and you say *¡Qué va!* that is a familiar way of saying 'No, no, I won't hear of it!' but if they say, 'He said he had dinner with the Duke of Medina Sidonia', and you said *¡Qué va!* it would mean 'I don't believe a word of it!' 'Nonsense!' is perhaps the easiest equation to remember.

¡Qué va! is often followed by *hombre*: Q. *¿No crees que molestará a tu esposa que vaya yo?* A. *¡Qué va, hombre! Le gustará mucho (el) verte.*

¡Vamos!, as a cliché, is said with a shrug of the shoulders (whether actual or implied) and means approximately 'after all!' In America the translation could be 'hell!' and it is inserted into the sentence in just the same way, e.g. 'I thought there'd be plenty but, hell, I didn't expect as much as this!' *Esperaba que hubiese mucho pero ¡vamos!, no tanto;* 'I tried to

prevent it but, after all, one can't be everywhere at once',
Quería impedirlo pero ¡vamos! no se puede estar en todo. It is,
however, much more common than either 'hell' or 'after all'
and its force is to cancel out what you have just said, e.g.
Q. 'Does it hurt?' A. 'Well, a bit, but nothing much'.
Q. *¿Te duele?* A. *Pues un poquito pero vamos.* . . . Sometimes
it would be the translation of 'What's the odds?' (Fr. *tant
pis*): *Es mucha molestia pero vamos* . . ., 'It's an infernal
nuisance, but there it is!' The best concept to bear in mind
is a shrug of the shoulders.

¡Vámonos! is simple enough. It means 'Let's go', from the
verb *irse*, and is a more convenient way of saying *Vamos
nos.* 'We ought to go' or 'It's time we went' would be
'*Tenemos que irnos*; *Vámonos* is less specific, it means 'Let's go'
or 'Here we go!' (Fr. *allons-y*).

¡Vaya! is the response to any surprising discovery or piece
of information and therefore equates with 'Go on!', 'You
don't say!', 'Fancy that!', or, as often as not, 'Blimey!' or 'Coo!'
or just 'Well!' At cards, for example, if a player, by not following suit, indicates that he has no trumps *¡Vaya!* would be an
appropriate exclamation. Sometimes the second *a* gets a
considerable accent—*¡Vayá!*—in just the same way as we
say 'Coo-er!' (but not the same accent; we drop our voice on
the '-er' and make it a low note whereas the -*á* is held at a
much higher, more interrogative pitch). It is, in any case,
not as vulgar as 'Coo-er!'

Another use of *vaya* is 'What a . . .!', e.g. *¡Vaya tiempo!*,
'What weather!' and you should note that the article is not
used in Spanish, i.e. you do not say *¡Vaya una mujer!* for
'What a woman!' but simply *¡Vaya mujer!* It is rather stronger
than *¡Qué mujer!*

vago. An Unreliable Friend; applied to things it means 'vague',
as in English, but applied to people it means 'lazy'. 'A vague
person' would be *una persona informal, imprecisa, etc.*

¡vale! No, it does not mean 'good-bye', it is part of the verb *valer*
and means 'O.K.', at any rate in many contexts, though there
is nothing slangy about it; 'that's right' or 'that's correct'
would often be the translation, though it cannot be used in all
cases where *está bien* would do. Remember that *valer* means
'to be worth' so that *vale* means 'it is worth it', i.e. 'it is exactly
right' or sometimes 'good enough!' A man, having counted
the change and found it to be correct, would say, *¡vale!*, i.e.
'that's right!'; a man choosing a screw, for example, out of a
mass of them, and finding one that will fit would say *éste vale*,
'this'll fit', 'this'll be all right'; or when a crane is lowering
some object which the crane-driver cannot see and a second
man is calling out instructions, the latter will say *Más, más
aún*, and finally *¡vale!*, i.e. 'More! a bit more', and finally
'O.K.', whereupon the crane-driver stops. *¿Vale esto?*, 'Will

this do?' The reply is, *Sí, vale,* 'Yes, this'll be all right'. It is quite hard to remember, as *valer* is another of the verbs which do not exist as such in English and it is therefore one of the acid tests as to how your Spanish is getting on.

¿Cuánto vale? is the normal expression for 'How much?' when you are buying something.

válvula (f). A valve (*v.* CARS).

vaso (m). The normal word for a 'glass' (i.e. to drink from) (*v.* DOM. APP.).

vela (f). Candle, and you are advised to keep a few on the premises (*v.* DOM. APP.).

velocidades (f). Speeds, but in a car it is the proper word for 'gears'. A more current, though slightly less accurate, word is *cambios.* A three-speed gear on a bicycle is: *Un cambio de tres velocidades.* Gears in the stricter sense of gear-teeth are called *engranajes* (*v.* CARS).

venir bien, no venir mal. 'To be not a bad idea'; *me vendría(n) bien* is quite a good translation of 'I could do with': *no me vendrían mal cien pesetas,* '100 pesetas would come in handy'. 'Come in', in this sense, is perhaps quite a good equivalent (*v.* also **importar**).

ventanilla (f). Literally 'little window' but used of ticket offices and the like, though a more colloquial word is **taquilla** (*q.v.*).

ventilador (m). Literally 'ventilator' and so applied, quite correctly and logically, to the fan behind the radiator (*v.* CARS).

¡ver, a! 'Let's see!' Many languages use the infinitive for a general not too peremptory imperative (e.g. the German *Umsteigen, bitte!,* 'All change, please!') and this means literally 'to see!' Various English translations are: 'Let's have a look!', 'May I see?' or 'Show me!' If you really wanted to be polite you could say *¿Se puede ver?,* and *¡A ver!* is somewhat more abrupt but nevertheless worth learning as a cliché. You tell the Customs officer that you have only got three pairs of silk stockings, two bottles of scent and one of *coñac,* and he says *¡A ver!* and proceeds to examine the contents of your suit-case.

Vamos a ver is more precisely 'Let's go and have a look!' though it is not merely colloquial. Under *según* I mentioned *Según vamos a ver en el próximo capítulo,* 'As we shall see in the next chapter'. *Vamos a ver* is often merely a stronger form of *¡A ver!,* 'Let's see'. It is used quite a lot in a metaphorical sense, e.g. in argument when someone says, 'Well, is this really so?' and proceeds to examine whether it is really so or not. 'Well, is this really so?' would be translated *Pues, vamos a ver,* i.e. 'Let us look into the matter'.

¿verdad? The nearest Spanish equivalent to the French *'n'est-ce pas?'* and so the equivalent of 'isn't it?', 'haven't they?', 'wasn't she?', 'don't we?', and all the innumerable permutations which English imposes on us according to context; and just as these interrogatives are often not strictly questions but simply indications of a desire not to seem too confident, so can *¿verdad?* be tacked on to sentences to indicate the same state of mind.

It can be used positively for a strong 'yes', though here it is more correct to use the whole phrase *Sí, es (la) verdad*, 'Yes, that's perfectly true' or the Irish 'That's the truth'.

verdura (f). Greens, vegetables (*v.* FOOD). They need not to be strictly green, since the word applies to carrots, turnips, etc., but if you mean dried vegetables such as haricot beans you use *legumbres*.

vergüenza (f). *Vergüenza* is 'shame' and *vergonzoso* is 'shameful', but it is incorrect to suppose that *¡Qué vergüenza!* is 'What a shame!' since this is virtually the same in English as 'What a pity!' (i.e. *¡Qué pena!*, *¡Qué lástima!*). *¡Qué vergüenza!* is 'What a scandal!' (Fr. *Quelle honte!*), 'How shameful!', 'How disgraceful!', 'Isn't it outrageous!'

Another cliché is *sinvergüenza*, and this, by now, is practically a noun, meaning 'shameless person'. My *chica*, when doing the shopping, used frequently to refuse to buy necessities if she thought the price excessive, on the grounds that the people who demanded such prices were *sinvergüenzas*. The last Mass on a Sunday morning, which is celebrated at 2 o'clock, and is usually the most crowded of all, is called *La misa de los sinvergüenzas*, i.e. those who have got up late. (N.B. It is masculine, *un sinvergüenza*, unless the shameless one happens to be a woman.)

verificar. An Unreliable Friend. In some cases it might be translated 'to verify' but the word literally means 'to make true' and therefore 'to carry out', 'to perform', 'to do', and four times out of five it is likely to be used in this sense: *Harán falta alrededor de tres semanas para verificar este trabajo*, 'It'll take about three weeks to do this work'; *Verifíquese la siguiente prueba . . .*, 'Carry out the following test . . .'.

The word is mentioned here so that you can be aware of its meanings and you are not really advised to use it. 'To verify' is best rendered by *comprobar* (i.e. literally 'to put to the test'), and if you want to say 'to carry out', then *llevar a cabo* or simply *hacer* are much to be preferred.

vestido (m). A dress as worn by a lady. It suggests a long, single garment and can, therefore, apply to a nightdress (*vestido de noche*) but it is always a female garment. Evening-dress is *traje de etiqueta*. 'To dress', *vestirse*.

viento (m). Literally wind, but used more particularly in music for wood-wind (*v.* MUSIC).

vinagre (m). Vinegar (*v.* FOOD).

viola (f). Viola (*v.* MUSIC).

violento. An Unreliable Friend; in a normal context it is likely
to mean 'violent', e.g. *La explosión fué muy violenta; Sufrió una
muerte violenta*, etc., but when applied to a state of affairs or
a state of mind it takes on the surprisingly different meaning
of 'embarrassed', e.g. *Fué una situación muy violenta,* 'It was a
very awkward situation'.

The use of the verb *ser* or *estar* may sometimes indicate
which sense is intended, e.g. *Era un hombre un poco violento*,
'He was rather a violent man', whereas *Estaba un poco violento*,
'He was a bit embarrassed'. If you feel disinclined to trust
yourself on such ground use *sentirse violento* for 'to feel
embarrassed'. Safer still, of course, is *confuso* for 'embarrassed'
and *confusión* for 'embarrassment'.

violín (m). Violin. **violoncello, violoncelo** or **violonchelo** (m).
Violoncello (*v.* MUSIC).

visto, por lo. Confronted with this phrase it is not difficult to
calculate that it means 'apparently', even if you did not know
it already, but it is another of those which are hard to remember to use. Other possible translations might be, 'I suppose so'
or 'presumably', but there are very few contexts where
'apparently' would not be perfectly correct and you may use
it at the end or the beginning of a sentence: *¿Va a venir? Sí,
por lo visto*, 'Is he coming? Yes, apparently', or *Por lo visto
no va a venir*, 'It looks as though he isn't coming'. 'By the
look of things' is quite a good basic concept.

Other clichés with *visto* are *bien visto* and *mal visto*, meaning
'the done thing' or 'chic' or 'popular', and 'not done' or
'unpopular', respectively (cf. Fr. *bien vu, mal vu*).

volante (m). Steering-wheel (*v.* CARS). Strictly speaking it is a
fly-wheel and is correct wherever fly-wheel is intended,
including the fly-wheel of a car. Its use for steering-wheel is
therefore a misnomer, but there it is!

volver, volverse, vuelta. You must know that this is the proper
word for 'to turn', 'to turn over', 'to return', 'to come back',
'to go back', etc., and I need do no more than remind you that
it is transitive as well as intransitive, e.g. *vuélvalo*, 'turn it
over' (the page, the record, etc.). Used in this way it is a
perfectly proper word and not colloquial.

Volverse is often rather more colloquial and its use more
idiomatic. It is one of the ways of handling 'to become': *Me
estoy volviendo loco*, 'I'm going crazy'.

The noun *vuelta* is very common and used in a good
many different senses. It is the straightforward word for
'change' (i.e. in connection with money): *Estoy esperando la
vuelta*, 'I'm waiting for my change'. In connection with a
gramophone record, or a coin or other two-sided article it
means 'the other side': *Pon la vuelta*, 'Put the other side on'

(i.e. of a gramophone). *Dar la vuelta* is decidedly worth bearing in mind as it is the commonest translation of 'to turn round' e.g. in a car: *Hay que dar la vuelta y volver*, 'We shall have to turn round and go back again'.

Dar una vuelta should be carefully distinguished from it as it means 'to take a turn', i.e. 'to take a little walk', 'to potter about in'; the 'in' being conveyed by *por*: *Voy a dar una vuelta por la calle*, 'I'm going to take a turn in the streets'.

voy. I use the first person singular as this is the commonest form. Obviously it means 'I go', but I am concerned with cases where it means 'I come'. Probably it has not occurred to you that when you say 'I'm coming' you are regarding the action from the other person's point of view; as far as you yourself are concerned, you are going and the Spaniards regard it this way. Thus, in a restaurant or café, when you call out 'Waiter!' (or say 'Ss-t', or clap your hands) the waiter will reply ¡*Voy!* (in other cases you may hear ¡*Va!* (i.e. he (she) is coming), which is nearly as common as *voy*) and the equation is 'Coming, sir!' Similarly when you ring up and say 'I shan't be coming home to lunch', the Spanish is *No voy a casa a comer*.

vulgar. Perhaps hardly deserving an entry but bordering on the Falso Amigo; it means 'popular' rather than 'vulgar', e.g. *Canciones vulgares*, 'Popular songs', a title that might be most misleading if you were not warned. It is true that if you call something *muy vulgar* in a derogatory tone of voice it has the connotation of 'vulgar' in the sense of 'common' but not of 'indecent'. *Vulgarización* is a definite Falso Amigo; it means 'popularisation' and suggests such things as Adult Education, i.e. raising the level of the lower classes, whereas 'vulgarisation' suggests dragging down the level of the upper.

If you want 'vulgar' in the sense of 'common' or 'rude' a better word is probably *ordinario*; if you mean 'indecent', say *indecente* or, more colloquially, *verde* (*un chiste verde* is 'a low story'); but if you mean a sort of general robust and lively, cheery, beery, slap-and-tickle, Villikins-and-his-Dinah vulgarity then use *vulgar* or *soez*.

vulnerable. Vulnerable, at bridge.

W

water (m). Obviously an importation from England; one of our less visible exports. It is short for 'water-closet' and is pronounced *váter*. Another, more properly Spanish, word is *retrete* (*q.v.*) (*v.* DOM. APP.).

Y

ya. One of the commonest words in the language and therefore extending some distance from the basic meaning of 'already'. Quite often the equation is simply 'yes' and you almost get the impression that German is being spoken, for example, when something is being explained to you and you already understand it you say, *Ya, ya, ya,* 'Yes, yes, I see' or ' . . . I know'; alternatively, when you suddenly tumble to it: 'Ah yes, I see!' would likewise be *¡Ah, ya!*; also when you are listening to a narration of something and wish to give an occasional, confirmatory 'yes' to show that you follow, you would say *Ya.*

Ya is also used a great deal in conjunction with various verbal expressions to indicate something approaching obviousness, e.g. *Ya lo sabes* or *Ya sabes,* 'You know that perfectly well'; *Ya lo sé,* 'Yes, yes, I know that' or just 'Yes, I know'; and a very common cliché is *¡Ya lo creo!* or *¡Hombre, ya lo creo!* which means 'I should say so!' or 'Good heavens, yes!' or the American 'I'll say!' or 'Rather!', 'I can well believe it'.

Sometimes the translation would be 'now', e.g. *Ya me voy,* 'I'll be off now'. There is a Christmas carol whose refrain runs: *Pastores venid, pastores llegad a adorar al niño que ha nacido ya,* and to account for this final *ya* I suppose we should say 'who is born today' i.e. another aspect of 'now'.

Ya que is the proper translation of 'since' or 'as' and is not necessarily colloquial; *ya que no hemos tenido noticias suyas,* 'as we have not heard from you'.

Generally speaking *ya* is a word whose use can only be learnt by experience since in many contexts we have no exact equivalent in English, e.g. *Ya es hora de que hubiera venido,* 'It's (high) time he was here'; in so far as *ya* is translated in this context it means 'high'. Similarly *¡Ya viene!,* 'Here he comes!' and the translation is then 'here'. No dictionary could teach you all such uses, you simply have to acquire the sense of obviousness or overdueness and slip it in. The proper use of it will serve as a measure of your progress in Spanish.

Z

zanahoria (f). Carrot (*v.* FOOD).

zapata (f). Brake-shoe (*v.* CARS).

zapatilla (f). Slipper. Note the gender.

zapato (m). Shoe.

zorros (m. pl.). This word applies to a bunch of rags (hence the plural form) tied to a stick and used for dusting ornate objects which are too complicated to be dusted in a straightforward manner. The technique is to flap around the object in question so as to remove the more obvious evidences of dust (*v.* DOM. APP.).

zurcir. To darn, to repair socks, stockings, etc. (*v.* DOM. APP.).

SPECIAL VOCABULARIES

FALSOS AMIGOS Y AMIGOS INFORMALES
(False Friends and Unreliable Friends)

English has absorbed so much Latin into its vocabulary that there are a great many words which, apart from minor differences of spelling, appear the same as their Spanish equivalents and are therefore presumed to have the same meaning. Very often this is so, e.g. *vocabulario*, 'vocabulary', *diferencia*, 'difference', etc., but almost as often it is not, and students would be well advised to assume them all guilty until they are proved innocent.

A False Friend is a case where the meaning is decidedly different, e.g. *decepción*, 'disappointment', not 'deception' which is *engaño*. An Unreliable Friend is one where the meaning is sometimes, but not always the same, e.g. *formal* (or *informal*) which may mean 'formal' (or 'informal') but most often means 'reliable' (or 'unreliable').

The following list is not intended to be exhaustive. It merely gives the commoner cases and is designed for ready reference or for memorising. A more detailed examination of the meanings will be found in the main text.

Spanish—English

actual, present (of time)
apuntar, jot down, make note of
asistir, attend, be present at
atender, to pay attention
bizcocho, sponge-cake
carpeta, file
carta, letter
cigarro, cigarette
conferencia, lecture, long-distance call, conference
constipado,(having)a cold
decepción, disappointment
desgracia, misfortune
desmayo, faint, swoon
dirección, address, steering, direction
distinto, different
embarazada, pregnant
emoción, excitement, emotion

éxito, success
expedir, send off
fábrica, factory

English—Spanish

actual, real, verdadero, efectivo
appoint, nombrar
assist, ayudar
attend, asistir
biscuit, galleta
carpet, alfombra
card, tarjeta
cigar, puro
conference, congreso, entrevista

constipated, estreñido
deception, engaño
disgrace, deshonra, vergüenza
dismay, descorazonamiento
direction, dirección

distinct, claro, visible
embarrassed, confuso
emotion, sentimientos, emoción
exit, salida
expedite, meter prisa
fabric, textíl, material

Spanish—English	*English—Spanish*
falta, default, lack	**fault**, culpa
flan, caramel custard	**flan**, torta
formal, reliable, formal	**formal**, formal, de formalidad
genial, having genius	**genial**, cordial, sociable, cariñoso
gracioso, witty	**gracious**, cortés, elegante
honesta, chaste	**honest**, honrado
ignorar, to be unaware	**ignore**, no hacerse caso
ingenioso, witty	**ingenious**, listo
largo, long	**large**, grande, amplio
lectura, reading	**lecture**, conferencia
matrícula, registration number	**matriculation** (no exact equivalent)
ordinario, rude, common, vulgar	**ordinary**, corriente, regular
plausible, praiseworthy, laudable	**plausible**, especioso
prevenir, to warn	**prevent**, impedir
probar, to try, to try out	**prove**, comprobar
prospecto, prospectus	**prospect**, futuro, perspectiva, panorama
quitar, to take away	**quit**, salir de
realizar, to achieve, to bring about	**realise**, darse cuenta
regular, so-so, all right	**regular** (see note)
sano, healthy	**sane**, cuerdo
sensible, sensitive, aware, conscious	**sensible**, práctico, sensato
simpático, nice, pleasant (of persons)	**sympathetic**, compasivo
suburbio, slum	**suburb**, afuera
sustraer, to deduce, to 'pinch' (steal)	**subtract**, restar
traducir, translate	**traduce**, calumniar, difamar
trasladar, to transfer, move	**translate**, traducir
vago (of persons), lazy	**vague** (of persons), informal, impreciso
verificar, carry out, perform	**verify**, comprobar
violento, embarrassing, violent	**violent**, violento
vulgarización, popularisation	**vulgarisation** (no precise word)

DISCONCERTING GENDERS

In the earlier stages of speaking Spanish one is tempted to put '*la*' before every word ending in 'a' and *el* before nearly everything else, except perhaps words ending in *-ión*. The following list is simply a reminder of some of the commoner words whose gender may take you unawares. There are many other less common words.

FEMININE which you might have expected to be masculine:

Spanish—English

La central, telephone exchange
La capital, capital city
La editorial, publishing house
La catedral, cathedral
La labor, work
La flor, flower
La red, network
La sed, thirst
La col, cabbage
La sal, salt
La piel, skin
La tos, cough
La vocal, vowel
La dínamo, dynamo
La foto, short for **fotografía**
La moto, short for **motocicleta**
La mano, hand
La radio, radio
La cárcel, prison
La sartén, frying-pan
La razón, reason
La crisis, crisis

MASCULINE which you might have expected to be feminine:

Spanish—English

el telegrama, telegram
el idioma, language
el problema, problem
el programa, program
el síntoma, symptom
el panorama, panorama
el sistema, system
el guardarropa, wardrobe
el clima, climate
el mapa, map
el sofá, sofa
el policía, policeman[1]
el guardia, policeman[1]
el día, day

Also most words ending in *-ista,* e.g. *artista, telefonista,* etc., provided the person concerned is male; if female they become feminine.

I do not need to remind you that such words as *el agua, el aria,* etc., are not really masculine; they take '*el*' in the singular form simply because they begin with an accented '*a*' and *la agua* would sound awkward.

---

[1] These are masculine only when they refer to the man. If *la policía* is used meaning the 'police force', or *guardia* meaning the 'guard' (i.e. of the sort which is changed at Buckingham Palace), then both become feminine.

CARS

accidente (m), accident
aceite (m), oil
acelerador (m), accelerator
acumulador (m), battery
aire (m), choke, air
aleta (f), fender
amortiguador (m), shock-absorber
aparcar, to park
árbol (de levas), camshaft
arrancar, to start up
arranque (m), self-starter
asiento (m), seat
auto (m), car
avería (f), breakdown

ballesta (f), spring (lamin.)
batería (f), battery
biela (f), connecting-rod
bloque (m), cylinder-block
bobina (f), coil, transformer
bocina (f), horn
bomba (f), pump
bombear, to pump
bujía (f), spark   plug

cadena (f), chain
caja de cambio (f), gear-box
cámara (f), inner-tube
cambios (m. pl.), 'gears'
camisa (f), cylinder-sleeve
capot (m), hood
carburador (m), carburetor
cárter (m), crankcase
chófer (m), chauffeur, driver
cigüeñal (m), crankshaft
cilindro (m), cylinder
claxón (m), horn
coche (m), car
condensador (m), condenser
conducir, to drive
correa (del ventilador), fan-belt
cruceta (f), universal joint

cubierta (f), tyre (outer cover)
cuentakilómetros, odometer

dar aire, to pump
dar la vuelta, to turn round
delco (m), distributor
depósito (m),   gas tank
despiste (m), skid
despistar, to skid
destornillador   (m),   screw-driver
diferencial (m), differential
dínamo (f), dynamo
dirección (f), steering
directa (f), top gear
disco de embrague (m), clutch disc

eje (m), axle
embrague (m), clutch
encendido (m), ignition
engranado, geared
engranaje (m), gearing
engrase (m), greasing, lubrication
escape (m), exhaust
escobilla (f), brush (dynamo)
estacionar, to park

faro (m), headlight
filtro (m), filter
flecha (f), trafficator, direction-indicator
frenar, to brake
freno (m), brake

garaje (m), garage
gasolina (f), petrol (Amer. gas)
gato (m), jack
grasa (f), grease
guardabarro (m), mudguard, fender

hinchar, to pump

jaula (f), lock-up garage

limpiaparabrisas (m), windscreen-wiper

líquido de frenos (m), brake fluid

luz de estacionamiento (f) sidelight

llave (f), wrench, key

manivela (f), cranking-handle
marcha atrás (f), reverse
martillo (m), hammer
matrícula (f), license plate
'moto' (f), motor-bike
motor (m), engine
muelle (m), spring (spiral)

neumático (m), tire

palanca (f), lever
palier (m), axle-shaft
panel (m), panel, dashboard
parabrisas (m), windscreen
parachoques (m), bumper
parar, to stop, to switch off
patinar, to skid
patinazo (m), skid
pedal (m), pedal
piloto (m), tail-lamp
pinchazo (m), puncture

pistón (m), piston
platino (m), contact-point
portaequipaje (m), trunk, **—jes**, luggage grid
puesta en marcha(f), selfstarter
punto muerto (m), neutral

radiador (m), radiator
(de) repuesto, spare
retén (m), oil-seal
rodamiento (a bolas), ballbearings
rueda (f), wheel
rueda de repuesto (f), spare wheel

segmento (m), piston-ring

tapa (f), cover, lid
tapacubos (m), hub cap
tornillo (m), screw, bolt
transmisión (f), transmission
tuerca (f), nut

válvula (f), valve
velocidades (f. pl.), 'gears'
ventilador (m), fan
volante (m), steering-wheel, fly-wheel

zapata (f), brake-shoe

English—Spanish

accelerator, acelerador (m)
accident, accidente (m)
accumulator, acumulador (m)
axle, eje (m)
axle-shaft, palier (m)

(ball) bearings, rodamiento (a bolas)
battery, batería (f)
bolt, tornillo (m)
bonnet, capot (m)
brake, freno (m)
to brake, frenar
brake fluid, líquido de frenos
brake-shoe, zapata (f)
breakdown, avería (f)

brush (dynamo), escobilla (f)
bumper, parachoques (m)

camshaft, árbol de levas (m)
car, coche, auto (m)
carburetor, carburador (m)
chain, cadena (f)
chauffeur, chófer (m)
choke, aire (m)
clutch, embrague (m)
clutch disc, disco de embr. (m)
coil, bobina (f)
condenser, condensador (m)
connecting-rod, biela (f)
contact-point, platino (m)
cover, tapa (f)

crankcase, cárter (m)
cranking-handle, manivela (f)
crankshaft, cigüeñal (m)
cylinder, cilindro (m)
cylinder-block, bloque (m)
cylinder-sleeve, camisa (f)

dashboard, cuadro de mandos (m)
differential, diferencial (m)
direction-indicator, flecha (f)
distributor, delco (m)
to drive, conducir
driver, chófer (m or f)
dynamo, dínamo (f)

engine, motor (m)
exhaust, escape (m)

fan, ventilador (m)
fan-belt, correa (f)
filter, filtro (m)
flipper, flecha (f)
fly-wheel, volante (m)
foot-brake, freno de pie (m)

garage, garaje (m)
'gas', gasolina (f)
gears, cambios, velocidades
geared, engranado
gearing, engranaje (m)
gear-box, caja de cambio (f)
grease, grasa (f)
greasing, engrase (m)

hammer, martillo (m)
hand-brake, freno a mano (m)
headlight, faro (m)
horn, bocina (f), claxon (m)
hub cap, tapacubos

ignition, encendido (m)
inner-tube, cámara (f)

jack, gato (m)

key, llave (f)

lever, palanca (f)
lid, tapa (f)

lock-up garage, jaula (f)
lubrication, engrase (m)
luggage-grid, portaequipajes (m)

milometer, cuentrakilómetros (m)
motor-bike, moto (f)
mudguard, aleta (f), guardabarro (m)

neutral, punto muerto (m)
number plate, matrícula (f)
nut, tuerca (f)

oil, aceite (m)
oil-seal, retén (m)

panel, panel (m)
to park, aparcar, estacionar
pedal, pedal (m)
petrol, gasolina (f)
petrol-tank, depósito (m)
piston, pistón (m)
piston-ring, segmento (m)
pump, bomba (f)
to pump, dar aire, hinchar
puncture, pinchazo (m)

radiator, radiador (m)
reverse, marcha atrás (f)

screw, tornillo (m)
screwdriver, destornillador (m)
seat, asiento (m)
self-starter, arranque (m), puesta en marcha (f)
shock-absorber, amortiguador (m)
sidelight, luz de estacionamiento (f)
skid, patinazo, despiste (m)
to skid, patinar
spare, de repuesto
spare-wheel, rueda de repuesto (f)
spark plug, bujía (f)
speedometer, indicador (de veloc.)

spring, ballesta (lamin., f) muelle (spiral, m)
to start up, arrancar
to steer, dirigir
steering, dirección (f)
steering-wheel, volante (m)
to stop, parar
to switch off, parar

tail-lamp, piloto (m)
top gear, directa (f)
transmission, transmisión (f)
to turn round, dar la vuelta

tyre, neumático (m), cubierta (f)

universal joint, cruceta (f)

valve, válvula (f)

wheel, rueda (f)
windscreen, parabrisas (m)
windscreen-wiper, limpia-parabrisas (m)
wing, aleta (f), guardabarro (m)

DOMESTIC APPURTENANCES

Spanish—English

aguja (f), needle
alfiler (m), pin
alfombra (f), carpet
algodón (m), cotton
almirez (m), mortar
almohada (f), pillow, cushion
apagar, to switch off
arandela (f), washer (in tap)
armario (m), cupboard
asperón (m), sand for cleaning
azulejo (m), tile

bandeja (f), tray
baño (m), bath
bayeta (f), floor-cloth
bidé (m), bidet
bombilla (f), electric bulb
butaca (f), arm-chair

cacerola (f), flat, open saucepan
cafetera (f), coffee-pot, kettle
cama (f), bed
cañería (f), drains
carrera (f), ladder (in stocking)
cazo (m), saucepan (one handle)
cazuela (f), earthenware dish
cepillo (m), brush
clavo (m), nail
cogedor (m), shovel, dustpan
contador (m), meter (gas or electricity)
cristal (m), glass, pane of glass
cubo (m), bucket, garbage can

destornillador (m), screwdriver

encender, to switch on, light
enchufar, to plug in
enchufe (m), electric plug
escoba (f), long-handled broom

espumadera (f), spatula for removing foam or scum
estera (f), mat
estropajo (m), fibre for washing up, dish-cloth

felpudo (m), fibre door-mat
fogón (m), stove, kitchen-range
fregadero (m), sink
fregar, to wash up
fuente (f), dish, platter

gamuza (f), shammy
grifo (m), tap, faucet

horno (m), oven

jarra (f) jar, **jarro** (m), jug

lampara (f), lamp, electric bulb
lana (f), wool
lavabo (m), wash-basin
lejía (f), chloride of lime (liquid) for washing purposes
loza (f), earthenware (in general)

mango (m), handle
mano de almirez (f), pestle
manta (f), blanket, rug
mantel (m), table-cloth
martillo (m), hammer

nevera (f), refrigerator, ice-box

olla (f), saucepan with two handles

palmatoria (f), candlestick
pila (f), sink
plancha (f), iron (also grill)
planchar, to iron
platillo (m), saucer

plato (m), dish (lit. and metaph.)
plumero (m), feather-duster

retrete (m), water-closet

sábana (f), sheet
sartén (f), frying-pan
seda (f), silk
silla (f), chair
sillón (m), arm-chair
sofá (m), sofa, divan
suelo (m), floor, ground

tapa, tapadera (f), lid

tapón (m), plug (of a basin)
taza (f), cup
tazón (m), china bowl
tenazas (f. pl.), pincers, pliers
tetera (f), tea-pot, kettle
tijeras (f. pl.), scissors
trapo (m), cloth, rag, duster
tubería (f), drains, pipes

vaso (m), (a) glass, tumbler
vela (f), candle

water (m), water-closet

zorros (m. pl.), flap duster
zurcir, to darn

English—Spanish

arm-chair, sillón (m), butaca (f)
ashet, fuente (f)

basin, tazón (m)
bath, baño (m)
bed, cama (f)
bidet, bidé (m)
blanket, manta (f)
bowl, tazón (n)
broom, escoba (f)
brush, cepillo (m)
bucket, cubo (m)
bulb (electric), bombilla (f)

candle, vela (f)
candlestick, palmatoria (f)
carpet, alfombra (f)
chair, silla (f)
chloride of lime (liquid), lejía (f)
cloth, trapo (m)
coffee-pot, cafetera (f)
cotton, algodón (m)
cup, taza (f)
cupboard, armario (m)
cushion, almohada (f)

to darn, zurcir
dish, fuente, cazuela (f), plato (m)
dish-cloth, estropajo (m)

divan, sofá (m)
door-mat, felpudo (m)
drains, tubería, cañería (f)
dustbin, cubo (m)
duster, trapo (m), gamuza (f)
dustpan, cogedor (m)

earthenware, loza (f)
electric bulb, bombilla, lámpara (f)
electric plug, enchufe (m)

feather-duster, plumero (m)
flap duster, zorros (m. pl.)
floor, suelo (m)
floor-cloth, bayeta (f)
to fry, freír
frying-pan, sartén (f)

gas, gas-ring, gas (m)
glass, cristal (m)
(a) glass, vaso (m)

hammer, martillo (m)
handle, mango (m)

ice-box, nevera (f)
iron, plancha (f)
to iron, planchar

jar, jarra (f), **jug**, jarro (m)

kettle, tetera, cafetera (f)
kitchen-range, fogón (m)

ladder (steps), escalera (f)
ladder (stocking), carrera (f)
lamp, lámpara (f)
to light, encender

mat, estera (f)
meter (gas or electricity), contador (m)
mortar, almirez (m)

nail, clavo (m)
needle, aguja (f)

oven, horno (m)

pane (of glass), cristal (m)
pestle, mano de almirez (f)
pillow, almohada (f)
pin, alfiler (m)
pincers, tenazas (f. pl.)
pipe, tubo (m)
pipes, tubería (f)
plate, plato (m)
plug (of a basin), tapón (m)
plug (electric), enchufe (m)
to plug in, enchufar

rag, trapo (m)
refrigerator, nevera (f)

saucepan, cazo (m), cacerola, olla (f)
saucer, platillo (m)
scissors, tijeras (f. pl.)
sheet, sábana (f)
shovel, cogedor (m)
silk, seda (f)
sink, fregadero (m), pila (f)
sofa, sofá (m)
spatula, espumadera (f)
staircase, escalera (f)
stove, fogón (m)
to switch on, encender
to switch off, apagar

table-cloth, mantel (m)
tap, grifo (m)
tea-pot, tetera (f)
tile, azulejo (m)
tray, bandeja (f)
tumbler, vaso (m)

wash-basin, lavabo (m)
washer (of a tap), arandela (f)
to wash up, fregar
water-closet, water (m), retrete (m)
wool, lana (f)

yellow duster, gamuza (f)

FOOD

aceite (m), olive oil
aceituna (f), olive
ahumado, smoked
almeja (f), cockle, clam
ajo (m), garlic
albaricoque (m), apricot
albóndiga (f), rissole
almendra (f), almond
anchoa (f), anchovy
apio (m), celery
arenque (m), herring
arroz (m), rice
asado, roast, baked
atún (m), tuna fish
ave (m), bird, poultry
avellana (f), hazel-nut

bechamela (f), white sauce
bonito (m), bonito
breva (f), black fig

cacahuete (m), peanut
calabacín (m), squash (veg.)
calamares (m. pl.), squids
caldo (m), thin soup, consommé
canela (f), cinnamon
cangrejo (m), crab
caracol (m), snail
carbonada (f), broiled meat
carne (f), meat
castaña (f), chestnut
cebolla (f), onion
cerdo (m), pork
cerezas (f. pl.), white cherries
champiñón (m), mushroom
chipirones (m. pl.), *v.* **calamares**
chirimoya (f), custard-apple
chirivía (f), parsnip
chucrut (m), sauerkraut
chuleta (f), cutlet, chop
cigala (f), 'langoustine'
ciruela (f), plum

clavo (m), clove
cochinillo (m), sucking pig
col (f), cabbage
coliflor (f), cauliflower
compota (f), marmalade
conservas (f. pl.), preserves
cordero (m), mutton

ensalada (f), salad, lettuce
ensaladilla (f), vegetable salad
entrecot (m), sirloin of beef
entremeses (m. pl.), hors d'œuvres
escabeche (m), tinned bonito
espada (f), swordfish
espárragos (m. pl.), asparagus
espinacas (f. pl.), spinach
estofado (m), stew

faisán (m), pheasant
fiambre (m), cold meat
flan (m), egg custard
frambuesa (f), raspberry
freír, to fry
fresa (f), wild strawberry
fresón (m), strawberry
frito, fried
fruta (f), fruit

gallina (f), chicken
gamba (f), prawn
garbanzo (m), chick pea
garni, with vegetables

grosella (f), red currant
guinda (f), black cherry
guisantes (m. pl.), peas (green)

helado (m), ice-cream
higo (m), fig
huevo (m), egg
huevos duros, hard-boiled eggs
huevos escalfados, poached eggs

huevos pasados por agua, boiled eggs
huevos al plato, shirred eggs
huevos revueltos, scrambled eggs
huevos rusos, egg mayonnaise

jamón (m), ham
jerez (m), sherry
judías (f. pl.), beans (green)

langosta (f), lobster
langostino (m), large prawn
lechal (m), sucking lamb
leche (f), milk
lechuga (f), lettuce
legumbres (m. pl.), dried vegetables (e.g. *garbanzos*)
lenguado (m), sole
limón (m), lemon
lubina (f), halibut

manteca (f), lard
mantecado (m), vanilla ice-cream
mantequilla (f), butter
manzana (f), apple
manzanilla (f), type of dry white sherry
mayonesa (f), mayonnaise
melocotón (m), cling peach
menta (f), mint
merluza (f), haddock
mermelada (f), jam (appr.)
mero (m), sea-bass
miel (f), honey
minuta (f), menu, bill of fare
molinera, 'meunière'
mora (f), blackberry
mostaza (f), mustard

nabo (m), turnip
naranja (f), orange
nata (f), cream
natilla (f), custard
nuez (f), walnut

oporto, port wine

paella (f), kedgeree (see note)
paraguaya (f), type of peach
parrilla (f), grill
pasas (f. pl.), raisins
pastel (m), cake
pastelería (f), pastries
patata (f), potato
pato (m), duck
pavo, pavipollo (m), turkey
pepino (m), cucumber
pera (f), pear
percebes (m. pl.), barnacles
perdiz (f), partridge
perejil (m), parsley
pescado (m), fish
pichón (m), pigeon
piña (f), pineapple
pisto (m) (see note)
platija (f), plaice
pollo (m), chicken
postre (m), sweet, dessert
puré, mashed

queso (m), cheese
quisquilla (f), shrimp

rebanada (f), slice
refresco (m), refreshment, snack, drink
remolacha (f), beets
rodaballo (m), turbot

sal (f), salt
salchicha (f), sausage
salchichón (m), type of 'salami'
salmón (m), salmon
salmonetes (m. pl.), whitebait
salsa (f), sauce
sardina (f), sardine
sidra (f), cider
solomillo (m), beef-steak, sirloin
sopa (f), thick soup
suizo (m), type of breakfast roll

tarta (f), tart
té (m), tea

ternera (f), veal
tinto, red (of wine)
tocino (m), bacon
tomate (m), tomato
tortilla (f), omelet
trucha (f), trout

tuétano (m), marrow (of bones)
uva (f), grape
verdura (f), vegetables (fresh)
vinagre (m), vinegar

zanahoria (f), carrot

English—Spanish

almond, almendra (f)
anchovy, anchoa (f)
apple, manzana (f)
apricot, albaricoque (m)
asparagus, espárragos (m. pl.)

bacon, tocino (m)
baked, asado
barnacles, percebes (m. pl.)
bass (sea), mero (m)
beans (green), judías (f. pl.)
beans (dried), judías secas (f. pl.)
beef-steak, solomillo (m)
beets, remolacha (f)
bill, cuenta (f)
blackberry, mora (f)
boiled eggs, huevos pasados
por agua
bonito, bonito (m)
bonito (tinned), escabeche (m)
butter, mantequilla (f)

cabbage, col (f)
cake, pastel (m)
carrot, zanahoria (f)
cauliflower, coliflor (f)
celery, apio (m)
cheese, queso (m)
cherry, cereza (f)
cherry (black), guinda (f)
chestnut, castaña (f)
chicken, pollo (m), gallina (f)
chop, chuleta (f)
cider, sidra (f)
cinnamon, canela (f)
clove, clavo (m)
cockles, almejas (f. pl.)
cold meats, fiambres (m. pl.)
crab, cangrejo (m)
crayfish, cangrejo de río
cream, nata (f)

cucumber, pepino (m)
custard, natilla (f)
custard-apple, chirimoya (f)
cutlet, chuleta (f)

dessert, postre (m)
duck, pato (m)

egg, huevo (m)
egg custard, flan (m)
egg mayonnaise, huevos rusos

fig, higo (m)
fig (black), breva (f)
fish, pescado (m)
fried, frito
fried eggs, huevos fritos
fruit, fruta (f)
to fry, freír

garlic, ajo (m)
ginger, gengibre (m)
grapes, uvas (f. pl.)
grill, parrilla (f)

haddock, merluza (f)
ham, jamón (m)
hard-boiled, duro
hazel-nut, avellana (f)
herring, arenque (m)
honey, miel (f)
hors d'œuvres, entremeses
(m. pl.)

ice-cream, helado, mantecado
(m)

jam, mermelada (f)

kedgeree, paella (f)

lamb, cordero lechal (m)
'langoustine', cigala (f)
lard, manteca (f)
lemon, limón (m)
lettuce, lechuga (f)
lobster, langosta (f)

marmalade, compota (f)
marrow (bone), tuétano (m)
marrow (vegetable), calabacín (m)
mashed, puré
mayonnaise, mayonesa (f)
meat, carne (f)
menu, minuta (f)
'meunière', molinera
milk, leche (f)
mint, menta (f)
mullet (red), lubina (f)
mushroom, champiñón, seta, hongo, etc.
mustard, mostaza (f)
mutton, cordero

olive, aceituna (f)
olive oil, aceite (m)
omelet, tortilla (f)
onion, cebolla (f)
orange, naranja (f)

parsley, perejil (m)
parsnip, chirivía (f)
partridge, perdiz (f)
pastries, pastelería (f)
peach, paraguaya (f)
peach (cling), melocotón (m)
peanut, cacahuete (m)
pear, pera (f)
peas, guisantes (m. pl.)
pheasant, faisán (m)
pigeon, pichón (m)
pineapple, piña (f)
plaice, platija (f)
plum, ciruela (f)
pork, cerdo (m)
port wine, oporto
potato, patata (f)
poultry, ave (m)

prawn, gamba (f)
preserves, conservas (f. pl.)

raisins, pasas (f. pl.)
raspberry, frambuesa (f)
red (of wine), tinto
red currant, grosella (f)
red mullet, lubina (f)
refreshment, refresco (m)
rice, arroz (m)
roast, asado

salad, ensalada (f)
salmon, salmón (m)
salt, sal (f)
sardine, sardina (f)
sauce, salsa (f)
sauerkraut, chucrut (m)
sausage, salchicha (f), salchichón (m)
scrambled eggs, huevos revueltos
sherry, jerez (m)
shrimp, quisquilla (f)
sirloin, entrecot (m)
slice, rebanada (f)
smoked, ahumado
snails, caracoles (m. pl.)
sole, lenguado (m)
soup (thin), caldo, consomé (m)
soup (thick), sopa (f)
spinach, espinacas (f. pl.)
squids, calamares, chipirones (m. pl.)
stew, estofado (m)
strawberry, fresón (m)
sucking pig, cochinillo (m)
sweet, postre (m)
sweet (adj), dulce
sweetbreads, lechecillas (f. pl.)
swordfish, espada (f)

tart, tarta (f)
tea, té (m)
tomato, tomate (m)
trout, trucha (f)
tuna fish, atún (m)

turbot, rodaballo (m)
turkey, pavo, pavipollo (m)
turnip, nabo (m)

veal, ternera (f)
vegetables (dried), legumbres
vegetables (fresh), verdura (f)

vegetable salad, ensaladilla (f)
vinegar, vinagre (m)

walnut, nuez (f)
whitebait, salmonetes (m. pl.)
white sauce, bechamela (f)
wild strawberry, fresa (f)

MUSIC

acento (m). accent
acorde (m), chord
alto, high (not contralto)
anacrusa (f), up-beat
aria (f), aria
arpa (f), harp
arpegio (m), arpeggio

bajo, bass
barra (f), bar-line
barras (f. pl.), double-bars
batuta (f), baton
bemol (m), flat (♭)
blanca (f), minim
bronce (m), brass

calderón (m), pause (⌢)
cello (m), cello (printed as in English)
clarinete (m), clarinet
clarinete bajo, bass clarinet
clave (f), clef
compás (m), bar (i.e. interval)
compás de primero, 1st time bar
compás de segundo, 2nd time bar
compás libre, a bar for nothing
contrabajo (m), double-bass
contrafagot (m), double bassoon
contralto (f), contralto
corchea (f), quaver
corno inglés (m), cor anglais
cuaternario (m), four-beat bar
cuerda (f), string, 'the strings'
¡cuidado! look out!

disonancia (f), discord
do, C (not doh)
dominante (f), dominant

empezar, to begin

escala (f), scale

fa, F (not fa)
fagot (m), bassoon
fermata (f), run
flauta (f), flute
fuerte, loud, strong
fusa (f), demi-semiquaver

glisado (m), run
grave, low, deep-toned

la, A (not lah)
lento, slow

llevar, to take (at a speed, etc.)

mayor, major
mediante (f), mediant
menor, minor
mi, E (not mi)
modulación (f), modulation
mordente (m), mordent, grace-note
movido, fast

natural, natural (♮)
negra (f), crotchet

oboe (m), oboe
octava (f), octave
otra vez, again

pedal (m), pedal
pentagrama (m), stave
percusión (f), percussion
piano, soft (also the instrument)
pistón (m), valve (of brass instrument)
platillo (m), cymbal
(con) prisa, fast
puntillo (m), dot
(con) puntillo, dotted

133

quinta (f), fifth

rápido, fast
re, D
recitativo (m), recitative
redonda (f), semibreve
registro (m), register

saxofón (m), saxophone
semicorchea (f), semiquaver
semifusa (f), demi-demi-semiquaver
semitono (m), semitone
sensible (f), leading-note
¡señores!, gentlemen!
si, B
silencio (m), rest (not pause)
sol, G (not soh)
solista (m or f), soloist
solistas, 'single desks'
solo, solo
soprano (f), soprano
sordino (m), mute
sostenido, sharp (♯)
sostenido, sustained
suave, soft
subdominante (f), sub-dominant

superdominante (f), super-dominant
supertónica, supertonic

tambor (m), side-drum
tecla (f), key (e.g. of a piano)
tenor, tenor
tercera (f), third
tiempo (m), beat, time, tempo, movement
timbal (m), kettledrum, 'timps'
tiple, treble, soprano
tocar, to play
tonalidad (f), key
tónica (f), tonic
tono (m), tone, pitch
tresillo (m), triplet
trino (m), trill
trombón (m), trombone
trompa (f), french horn
trompeta (f), trumpet
tuba (f), tuba

viento (m), wood-wind
viola (f), viola
violín (m), violin
violoncello, **violoncelo** or **violonchelo** (m), violoncello

English—Spanish

A, la
accent, acento (m)
again, otra vez
aria, aria (f)
arpeggio, arpegio (m)

B, si
bar, compás (m)
bar for nothing, compás libre
bar-line, barra (f)
bass, bajo
bass clarinet, clarinete bajo
bassoon, fagot (m)
baton, batuta (f)
beat, tiempo (m)
begin, empezar
bow (of violin, etc.), arco (m)
brass, bronce

C, doh
cello, cello (m)
chord, acorde (m)
clef, clave (f)
contralto, contralto (f)
cor anglais, corno inglés (m)
crotchet, negra (f)
cymbal, platillo (m)

D, re
demi-demi-semiquaver, semifusa (f)
discord, disonancia (f)
dominant, dominante (f)
dot, puntillo (m)
dotted, con puntillo
double-bars, barras (f. pl.)
double-bass, contrabajo (m)

double bassoon, contrafagot (m)

E, mi

F, fa
fast, movido, rápido, con prisa
fifth, quinta (f)
first-time bar, compás de primero
flat, bemol
flat (in pitch), bajo
flute, flauta (f)
four-beat bar, cuaternario (m)

G, sol
gentlemen!, ¡señores!

harp, arpa (f)
high, alto
horn, trompa (f)

kettledrum, timbal (m)
key, tonalidad (f)
key (of an instrument), tecla (f)

leading-note, sensible (f)
look out!, ¡cuidado!
loud, fuerte, forte
low, grave, bajo

major, mayor
mediant, mediante (f)
minim, blanca (f)
minor, menor
modulation, modulación (f)
mordent, mordente (f)
movement, tiempo (m)
mute, sordino (m)
muted, con sordino

natural, natural

oboe, oboe (m)
octave, octava (f)

pause, calderón (m)
pedal, pedal (m)

percussion, percusión (f)
piano, piano
pitch, tono (m)
to play, tocar

quaver, corchea (f)
quiet, suave

recitative, recitativo (m)
register, registro (m)
rest, silencio (m)
run, fermata (f), glisado (m)

saxophone, saxofón (m)
scale, escala (f)
second-time bar, compás de segundo
semibreve, redonda (f)
semiquaver, semicorchea (f)
semitone, semitono (m)
sharp (♯), sostenido (m)
sharp (adj), alto
side-drum, tambor (m)
'single desks', solistas
soft, suave
solo, solo
soloist, solista (m or f)
soprano, soprano (f)
stave, pentagrama (m)
strings, cuerda (f)
strong, fuerte
subdominant, subdominante (f)
sustained, sostenido
superdominant, superdominante (f)
supertonic, supertónica (f)

to take (at a speed), llevar
tenor, tenor
third, tercera (f)
time, tiempo (m)
'timps', timbal (m)
tone, tono (m)
tonic, tónica (f)
trill, trino (m)
triplet, tresillo (m)
trombone, trombón (m)
trumpet, trompeta (f)
tuba, tuba (f)

up-beat, anacrusa (f)

valve (of brass instrument), pistón (m)

viola, viola (f)

violin, violín (m)

violoncello, violoncello (m), violoncelo or violonchelo

wood-wind, viento (m)

CLICHÉS

'Gentlemen! I want to start with the second (third) movement', *¡Señores! quiero empezar con el segundo (tercer) tiempo.*

'I'm going to take it at one (two, three, four, six) in a bar', *Voy a llevarlo a uno (dos, tres, cuatro, seis).*

'Very quietly please', *Muy suave, por favor.*

'I'll give you a bar for nothing', *Les doy un compás libre.*

'Go back to the double-bar', *Vuelvan a las barras.*

'Go back to the change of key', *Vuelvan al cambio de tonalidad.*

'A little faster', *Un poco más movido.*

'The semiquavers need to be better articulated', *Hay que articular más las semicorcheas.*

'Don't forget the pause', *No hay que olvidar el calderón.*

'Take it again', *Otra vez.*

OFFICE APPURTENANCES

acento (m), accent
albarán (m), invoice, delivery note
archivador (m), filing-cabinet
archivar, to file
archivero, -a, filing-clerk
archivo, filing-room
'los archivos', 'the files'

bandeja (f), tray
barra (f), bar, stroke (typing)
botones (m), messenger
buró (m), roll-top desk

caja (f), cash-desk
caja fuerte (f), safe, strong-box
cajero, -a, cashier
carpeta (f), file
central (f), telephone exchange
centralita (f), private exchange
chincheta (f), drawing-pin, thumb-tack
cinta (f), ribbon, tape
cliché (m), stencil
clip (m), paper-clip
cobrador, (see note under **cobrar**)
coma (f), comma
comillas (f. pl.), inverted commas
contabilidad (f), accounts
contable (m or f), accountant
copia (f) (carbon) copy
cortapapeles (m), paper-knife

despacho (m), office (private)
dictar, to dictate
dos puntos, colon

encabezamiento (m), heading
en paréntesis, in brackets
envío (m), despatch
escribir (a máquina), to type
espaciador (m), space-key

expedir, to send off

factura (f), bill, invoice
ficha (f), card (of index)
fichero (m), card-index

giro postal (m), postal order
grapa (f), paper-fastener
guión (m), hyphen, dash (see note)

máquina de direcciones (f), addressograph
máquina de escribir (f), typewriter
mecanógrafa (m or f), typist
mesa (f), desk, table
multicopista(m), duplicator

oficina (f), office (general)

papel carbón (m), carbon paper
párrafo (m), (a) paragraph
pisapapeles (m. s. pl.), paper-weight
pluma (f), pen
plumilla (f), nib
punto (m), full stop
punto y coma, semicolon
punto y aparte, 'paragraph' (see note)

recoger, to collect, pick up (v. note)
regla (f), ruler
rodillo (m), roller (e.g. of typewriter)

secante (m), blotting paper
sobre (m), envelope

taladrar, to punch
taladro (m), (a) punch

taquigrafía (f), shorthand
taquígrafo, -a, shorthand-typist
taquilla (f), guichet, ticket-office
tecla (f), key (of typewriter)

tijeras (f. pl.), scissors
tinta (f), ink
tinta china, India ink

ventanilla (f), guichet, ticket-office window

English—Spanish

accent, acento (m)
accountant, contable (m or f)
accounts, contabilidad (f)
addressograph, máquina de direcciones (f)

bar (in typing), barra (f)
bill, factura (f)
blotting paper, secante (m)
bracket, paréntesis (f)
in brackets, en paréntesis

carbon paper, papel carbón (m)
card (of index), ficha (f)
card-index, fichero (m)
cash, moneda (f)
cash-desk, caja (f)
cashier, cajero, -a
to collect, recoger
colon, dos puntos
comma, coma (f)
inverted commas, comillas (f. pl.)
copy, copia (f).

dash (hyphen), guión (m)
desk, mesa (f)
despatch, envío (m)
to despatch, expedir
dictate, dictar
drawing-pin, chinche (ta)(f)
duplicator, multicopista (m)

envelope, sobre (m)

file, carpeta (f)
to file, archivar
'the files', 'los archivos'
filing-cabinet, archivador (m)

filing-clerk, archivero, -a (m or f)
filing-room, archivo
full-stop, punto (m)

guichet, taquilla, ventanilla (f)
guide (telephone), guía (f)
guide (e.g. guide sheet), guión (m)

heading, encabezamiento (m)
hyphen, guión (m)

India ink, tinta china (f)
ink, tinta (f)
inverted commas, comillas (f. pl.)
invoice, albarán (m), factura (f)

key (of typewriter), tecla (f)

message, recado (m)
messenger, botones (m)
money order, giro postal (m)
nib, plumilla (f)

office (general), oficina (f)
office (private), despacho (m)

paper, papel (m)
paper-clip, clip (m)
paper-fastener, grapa (f)
paper-knife, cortapapeles (m)
paper-weight, pisapapeles (m)
paragraph, párrafo (m)
'paragraph', punto y aparte
to 'pick up', recoger
postal order, giro postal (m)
punch, taladro (m)
to punch, taladrar

ribbon (typewriter), cinta (f)
roller, rodillo (m)
roll-top desk, buró (m)
ruler, regla (f)

safe, caja fuerte (f)
scissors, tijeras (f. pl.)
semicolon, punto y coma
to send off, expedir
shorthand, taquigrafía (f)
shorthand-typist, taquígrafo, -a
space-key, espaciador
stencil, cliché (m)

stroke (typewriter), barra (f)
strong-box, caja fuerte (f)

telephone, teléfono (m)
telephone exchange, central (f)
telephone exchange (private), centralita (f)
thumb-tack, chinche (f)
ticket-office, taquilla (f)
tray, bandeja (f)
to type, escribir (a máquina)
typewriter, máquina (de escribir)
typist, mecanógrafo, -a

PLAYING CARDS

Spanish—English

apostar, to stake
¿a qué pinta?, What are trumps?
as (m), ace

banca (f), bank .
baraja (f), pack, deck
barajar, to shuffle, to make
bastos (m. pl.), clubs (Spanish)
baza (f), trick
bola (f), grand slam

caballo (m), knight (Spanish, queen)
carta (f), card
comodín (m), joker
copas (f. pl.), hearts (Spanish)
corazones (m. pl.), hearts
cortar, to cut

dar, to deal
diamantes (m), diamonds
doblar, to double

espadas (f. pl.), spades

fallar, to fail to follow suit, to trump
figura (f), face card

ganar, to win

honor (m), honour

juego (m), rubber (not game) (bridge)

jugar, to play

manga (f), game (in bridge)
mano (f), the person who leads
marcar, to bid (in bridge)
media bola (f), little slam
muerto (m), dummy

naipe (m), card
nulos, misère

oros (m), diamonds (Spanish)

palo (m), suit
'paso', (I) pass, no bid
puente (f), bridge (more often *brich*)
punto (m), point

redoblar, to re-double
reina (f), queen
repartir, to deal
rey (m), king

sin triunfos, no trumps
slam (m), slam
sota (f), knave, jack

tener la banca, to be banker
tener la mano, to be person who leads
trébol, clubs
triunfo (m), trump

English—Spanish

ace, as (m)

bank, banca (f)
to be banker, tener la banca
to bid, marcar (bridge)

'no bid', paso
bridge, bridge (pronounced *brich*), puente (f)

card, carta (f), naipe (m)

clubs, trébol (m)
clubs (Spanish), bastos (m. pl.)
court card, figura (f)
to cut, cortar

to deal, dar, repartir
deck, baraja (f)
diamonds, diamantes
diamonds (Spanish), oros
to double, doblar
dummy, muerto

to fail to follow suit, fallar

'game' (bridge), manga (f)
grand slam, bola (f)

hearts, corazones
hearts (Spanish), copas
honour, honor (m)

jack, sota (f)
joker, comodín (m)

king, rey (m)
knave, sota (f)
knight (Spanish), caballo (m)

to lead (i.e. be person who leads), tener la mano

little slam, media bola (f)

to make (shuffle), barajar
misère, nulos

pack, baraja (f)
'pass', paso
to play, jugar
point, punto (m)

queen, reina (f)

to re-double, redoblar
rubber, juego (m)

to shuffle, barajar
slam, slam (m)
spades, espadas (f. pl.)
to stake, apostar
suit, palo (m)

trick, baza (f)
trump, triunfo (m)
'no trumps', sin triunfos

'what are trumps?', ¿a qué pinta?
to win, ganar

NOTE: Spanish playing-cards are slightly different from those used elsewhere. The suits have different names, with the exception of spades, viz. Spades, *espadas*; Hearts, *copas*; Diamonds, *oros*; Clubs, *bastos*. In place of a Queen the Spaniards have a *Caballo* (Knight). The differences are not important and the same games could be played with either, but in practice Spaniards, when playing bridge, mostly use normal Western packs and often the English terminology as well, e.g. 'slam' instead of *bola*, 'game' instead of *manga*, etc.

TELEPHONES

'al habla', 'speaking'
auricular (m), earpiece

central (f), exchange
centralita (f), private exchange
colgar, to hang up (receiver)
comunicando, engaged, busy
conferencia (f), toll call
confundido, 'wrong number'

descolgar, to pick up
(receiver)
'dígame', 'hello' (*v.* note)
disco (m), dial

¿está Fulano?, Is So-and-So
there?

ficha (f), dummy coin

llamada (f), (a) call, ring

llamar, to ring up, to call

marcar (un número), to dial
(a number)
micrófono (m), mouthpiece

número (m), number

'¡oiga!', 'hello' (*v.* note)

poner (con), to put through
(to)

ranura (f), slot
recado (m), message

señal (f), signal, dialling tone
sonar, to ring (i.e. sound)

tono (m), dialling tone

call, llamada (f)
to call, llamar

dial, disco (m)
to dial, marcar
dialling tone, tono, señal (f)
dummy coin, ficha (f)

earpiece, auricular (m)
engaged, comunicando
exchange, central (f)
exchange (private), centralita
(f)

'hello', dígame, ¡oiga! (*v.* note)
to hang up, colgar

is So-and-So there?, ¿está
Fulano?

message, recado (m)
mouthpiece, micrófono (m)

number, número (m)

to pick up (receiver), descolgar
to put through (to), poner
(con)

to ring, sonar
to ring up, llamar

signal, señal (m)
slot, ranura (f)
'speaking', 'al habla', 'soy yo'

toll call, conferencia (f)

wrong number, confundido

CLICHÉS

Se ha confundido el número, Sorry, wrong number.
Póngame con el Señor . . ., Put me through to Mr. . . .
Quería hablar con . . . I wanted to speak to. . . .
Está comunicando,   Busy, sorry.
¿Quiere Vd. colgar, por favor?, Will you ring off (hang up) please.
No cuelgue, Don't ring off.
Dígame, Oiga, Hello (see notes).
¿Está el Señor . . .?, Is Mr. . . there?
¿De parte de quién?, Who is it speaking?
Le pongo en seguida, I'm just putting you through.
No está, He (she) isn't here.
¿Quiere Vd. dejar un recado?, Do you want to leave a message?
Tengo que colgar, I shall have to ring off.
Llamaré más tarde, I'll call again later.
Quiero poner una conferencia, I want to put through a toll   call.

NOTE: Spaniards do not use the international word 'hello' or 'allo' on the telephone; they use either *Diga* or *Oiga* and the notes under these words should be consulted.

The translation of 'Is So-and-So there' is not *¿Está Fulano allí?* but simply *¿Está Fulano?* The 'there' is not translated.

ENGLISH—SPANISH
Cross-reference Index

IMPORTANT NOTE: *The words 'cross-reference' cannot be too strongly emphasised.* The Spanish words in the following pages merely indicate the word to be looked up in the main Spanish-English section, where all commentary appears, and must not be taken as translations of the English words; in many cases that is exactly what they are not.

A (music), la
about, alrededor, eso
absent-minded, despistar
absolutely, completo, absoluto
accelerator, acelerador
accent, acento
accident, accidente
according to, según
account, cuenta
accounts, contabilidad
accustomed to, to be, soler
ace, as
acquire, to, proporcionar
actual, actual
address, dirección, señas
addressograph, máquina
affected, cursi
affection, cariño
afraid, miedo
after all, vamos
after you, pase
   some time after, pico
afternoon, good, tarde
afterwards, luego
again, otro
ago, a long while, rato
agree, acuerdo, conforme, quedar
agreement, acuerdo, conforme
air, aire
alike, parecido
all, not at-, nada
all right, confianza, convenir, dar, regular, nada
all's well, nada

almond, almendra
alone, to leave, soltar
always, soler
amused, -ing, divertido, gracia
anchovy, anchoa
angry, to be, echar
animated, movido
annoyed, fastidiado
another, otro
   and another thing, además
anyway, maneras, menos
appalling, asqueroso
apparently, al, visto
appear, cara, parecer
apple, manzana
apply oneself to, to, fijarse
appoint, apuntar
appointment, quedar
appreciable, apreciable
arm-chair, butaca
arrange, -ment, arreglar, concretar
arrival, on, al
as, como, según, ya que
as ... as, hasta
   as ... as that, eso, esto
   as if, plan
   as if, to look, cara, sonar
ascend, subir
ashet, fuente
asparagus, espárragos
assist, atender, asistir
atmosphere, ambiente
attaché-case, cartera

attempt, intentar
attention, to pay, atender, cuidado, caso, fijarse
aubergine, berenjena
audience, público
average, medio
away, to take, quitar, restar
awful, barbaridad, miedo
awful people, gente
awkward, violento
axis, axle, eje
axle-shaft, palier

B (music), si
bacon, tocino
bad, not, regular, venir bien
bad, just too, remedio
bad-tempered, genio
baked, asado
ball-bearings, rodamiento
band, cinta
bank, banca
banker, to be, tener
bar, barra, compás
bass, bajo
bass clarinet, clarinete
bassoon, fagot, bajón
bath, baño
baton, batuta
battery, batería
beam, manga
bean, garbanzo, judías
bearings, rodamiento
beat (music), tiempo, compás
beautiful, mona
beauty, you're a, anda
become, to, convertirse, hacerse, salir, llegar, ponerse, volverse
become of, to, pasar
bed, cama
beef-steak, entrecot, solomillo
beetroot, remolacha
beg, ruego
begin, empezar
believe, would you — it?, parecer: don't — a word of it, va
besides, además, inclusive

best, the — thing, mejor, indicado; do the best one can, tirar
bet, to, apostar
better, hay, tener que, indicado
bewildered, despistar
bid, to, marcar, subastar
bidet, bidé
big bug, categoría
bill, cuenta, factura
binge, juerga
bird, ave
biscuit, galleta
bit, and a—, pico
blackberry, mora
black cherry, guinda
blame, culpa
blanket, manta
bless you!, Dios, Jesús
'blessed', eso
'blimey!', vaya
block, bloque, manzana
blocked up, cañería
bloke, chico, tío
blotting paper, secante
blush, ponerse
bolt, tornillo
bones, no—broken, nada
bonito (tinned), escabeche
bonnet, capot
bore, boring, aburrido, fastidiado
bother, molestar
bounder, vergüenza
bowl, cazuela, tazón
box-office, taquilla
boy, chico
braces, tirantes
bracket, paréntesis
brains, sesos
brake, freno
  put brake on, to, echar
  fluid, líquido
  -shoe, zapata
branch, empalme
brass, bronce
brassière, sostén
brawl, jaleo
brazen, caradura

break, descanso
breakdown, avería
bring off, to, realizar
broom, escoba
browned off, fastidiado, harto
brush, cepillo
brush (elec.), escoba
bucket, cubo
bug, chincheta
bulb (elec.), bombilla, lámpara
bulb (plants), cebolla
bumper, parachoques
business, trabajo
but, sino
butter, mantequilla
'buttons', botones
by the way, paréntesis, propósito

C (music), do
cabbage, col
cage, jaula
cake, pastel
call, llamada
camshaft, árbol
can, bote, lata
candle, vela
candlestick, palmatoria
car, auto, coche
caramel custard, flan
carbon paper, papel
carburetor, carburador
card, carta, naipe, ficha
card-index, fichero
care, careful, ¡cuidado!
    couldn't — less, igual
carpet, alfombra
carrot, zanahoria
carry on, seguir
carry out, verificar, realizar
case, caso
    in any, maneras
    just in, acaso
cash, to, cobrar
cash-desk, caja
cauliflower, coliflor
celery, apio
cello, cello
certainly, caber, seguro

certainly is, hombre
    certainly not!, hablar
chain, cadena
chair, silla
chance, by any, acaso
change (money), volver
chap, chico, tío
    my dear —!, ¡hijo!
charitable, cariñoso
charming, encantado, precioso
chaste, honesto
chat, chatter, charla
chauffeur, chófer
cheek, what —!, caradura, fresco
cheese, queso
cheesed off, fastidiado, harto
cherry, cereza, guinda
chestnut, castaña
chi-chi, cursi
chic, visto
chicken, pollo, gallina
chicken-hearted, gallina
choke, aire
chord, acorde
    that strikes a —, sonar
chuck, echar, tirar
cigar, puro
cigarette, cigarro, pitillo
cigarette-lighter, mechero
clarinet, clarinete
clear, to get — of, soltar
clef, clave
clever, hacha, listo
clip, clip
cloth, trapo
clove, clavo
clubs (cards), trébol, bastos
clue, haven't a —!, absoluto
clutch, embrague
coarse, feo
cobbler, cordero
coffee-pot, cafetera
colander, colador
cold, to have a —, constipado
    to catch —, coger
collar, cuello
collect, to, recoger
colon, dos puntos
comb, peine

come in!, adelante, pase
  off, éxito
  on!, anda, hombre
  out, salir
  away, quitarse
  in handy, to, venir bien
  here he —!, ya
coming!, voy
  I'm not coming, voy
comma, coma
common, ordinario, vulgar
compass, compás
completely, completo
compliments, piropo
concentrate on, to, fijarse
condenser, condensador
conductor, cobrar, conducir
confidence, confianza
confused, embarazada, violento
congratulations, enhorabuena
congress, conferencia
connecting-rod, biela
consequently, resultar
constipated, constipado
contact, enchufar
continue, seguir
contralto, alto, contralto
contrive, to, conseguir
convenient, convenir
coo!, anda, hombre
cool, fresco
copy, copia
cor anglais, corno inglés
cord, cuerda
corkscrew, sacar
corner, esquina
counterfoil, ficha
course, of, claro, desde
  luego
  of — not!, hablar
court card, figura
coward, gallina
crab, cangrejo
crankcase, cárter
cranking-handle, manivela
crankshaft, cigüeñal
crawfish, crayfish, cangrejo,
  gamba
crazy, I'm going —, volver
cream, nata

crotchet, negra
crowd, gente
cuff-links, gemelos
cunning, listo
cup, taza
current, actual, corriente
curse, lata
cushion, almohada
custard, natilla
custard-apple, chirimoya
cut, cut off, out, away, etc.,
  cortar
cutlet, chuleta
cylinder, cilindro
cylinder-block, bloque
cylinder-sleeve, camisa
cymbal, platillo

D (music), re
dance, have a — with,
  sacar
darling, cariño
darn, to, zurcir
dash, guión
dashboard, salpicadero, panel
date, to have a — with,
  quedar
day, the other —, otro
dead earnest, broma
deadlock, punto muerto
deal, to, repartir, dar
Dear, my dear (letters),
  querer
deceive, decepción
decide, quedar
deduce, deduct, restar
deep, grave
default, falta
delicatessen, ultramarinos
delighted, encantado
delightful, precioso
demi-semiquaver, fusa
depends, it all —, según
deposit, fianza, depósito
deprive, quitar
desk, mesa
despatch, envío
despatch-case, cartera
dessert, postre

dial (telephone), disco
dial, to —, marcar
diamonds, diamantes, oros
dictate, to, dictar
difference, what — does it
make?, dar
different, distinto
differential, diferencial
difficult, to make, dificultar
dinner, comida
dinner-jacket, traje
direction-indicator, flecha
disappointed, -ment, decepción, disgustado
discord, disonancia
discover, enterarse, encontrar
disgraceful, vergüenza
disgusted, disgustado
disgusting, barbaridad
dish, fuente
dish-cloth, estropajo, trapo
dish out, to, repartir
distinct, distinto
distributor, delco
disturbance, trastorno
do, to, verificar, realizar
to — with, importar, venir
bien
please —!, Dios, falta
— come!, encantado
this'll —, convenir, vale
done, the — thing, visto
door-mat, felpudo
dot, puntillo
double-bars, barra
double-bass, contrabajo
double bassoon, contrafagot
double-spacing, espaciador
doubt, no doubt, caber,
seguro
down to, to get, liarse
drains, cañería, alcantarillas
draw, to, tirar
drawing-pin, chincheta
dress, vestido
dressing-gown, batín
drive, to, conducir
duck, pato
dummy (bridge), muerto
dummy coin, ficha

duplicator, multicopista
dustbin, cubo
duster, gamuza, plumero,
trapo, zorros
dustpan, cogedor

E (music), mi
earnest, dead, broma
earpiece, auricular
ear-rings, pendientes
earthenware, loza
eel, anguila
effective, hacha
egg, huevos
egg custard, flan
eject, echar
elder, mayor
elegant, mona
electric bulb, bombilla
elicit, sacar
embarrassed, violento
emerge, salir
emit, echar
emotion, emoción
engaged (telephone), comunicando
engine, motor
enrol, matrícula
envelope, sobre
even, not, ni siquiera
evening-dress, vestido, traje
evening, good, noche, tarde
events, at all —, maneras
evidently, visto
exchange (tel.), central
excite, -ment, emoción
don't get excited!, quieto
excuse me, favor
exhaust, escape
exhibit, enseñar
exit, éxito
expect, to, esperar
I — so, mejor
expedite, expedir
exploit, aprovechar
extra, sobrar, reserva
extract, to, sacar
extraordinary, isn't it —!,
parecer

F (music), fa
fabric, fábrica
facilitate, facilitar
factory, fábrica
fail, fallar
faint, desmayo
fair-to-middling, regular
fall short, fallar
family, in the — way, embarazada
fan-belt, correa
fancy that!, ¡vaya!
fast, movido, prisa
fastener (paper), grapa
fate, sino
faucet, grifo
fault, culpa, falta, remedio
fear, miedo
  no fear, hablar
fearful, barbaridad, miedo
feather-duster, plumero
feature, señas
fed up, disgustado, fastidiado, harto
feel, to — like, ganas
feelings, emoción
fellow, chico, tío
fend for oneself, to, tirar
'fiddle', trampa
fig, higo, breva
fifth, quinta
file, filing, archivo, carpeta
filter, filtro
filthy, asqueroso
find, to, encontrar, proporcionarse
  to — out, enterarse
'first house', tarde
fish out, to, sacar
fit, to, caber, convenir, vale
fix, to — up, arreglar, concretar
flat (music), bemol
flat (dwelling), piso
'flipper', flecha
floor, piso, suelo
floor-cloth, bayeta
flute, flauta
fly-wheel, volante
follow, to, entender, seguir

fond, to be — of, cariño
fool, hijo
foot, on, andar
for all the world, plan
forget, to, cuenta, echar
fork, empalme
formal, formal
'forties', tantos
fortunately, desgraciadamente
forward, adelante
French horn, trompa
frequently, menudo
fresh, fresco
Friday the 13th, martes
fried, frito
fright, susto
frightful, miedo, asqueroso
frightfully . . .!, (see Superlative, p. 13)
front, in, adelante
frying-pan, sartén
full-stop, punto
full-up, completo
fun, broma
funny, chiste, raro
  how —!, cosa
furious, to be, echar
further on, allá
fuss, trastorno

G (music), sol
game, juego
game (bridge), manga
garage, garaje, jaula
garlic, ajo
gas, gas
'gas', to, charla
gasoline, gasolina
gear, gearing, engranado, cambios, velocidades
gear-box, caja
gear-handle, palanca
general store, tienda
genius, genial
get, to, coger, conseguir, meterse, ponerse, salir
  along all right, tirar
  — clear of, to, soltar
  do you — me?, coger

get down to, to, liarse
for, to, proporcionar
hold of, to, conseguir, facilitar, proporcionar
I — it!, caigo, ya
into, meterse
on with it!, anda
on well, éxito
out, sacar, salir
out of, to, quitarse
something away, to, quitar
stuck into, liarse
ghastly, asqueroso, miedo
giddy, mareado
ginger, gengibre
glass, vaso, cristal
go, to, andar, va
on, to, pasar, seguir, vaya
up, to, subir
have a — at, intentar
here we go!, vámonos
let — of, to, soltar
let's —!, vámonos
God, Dios
for —'s sake!, Dios, hombre
my — no!, hablar
going, to get —, liarse
good-bye, hasta, adiós
good enough, vale
good enough to, amable, favor
evening, noches, tarde
-natured, simpático, cariñoso
heavens!, Dios, hablar, hombre
heavens, no!, hablar
goodness, thank!, menos mal
gorgeous, estupendo
gossip, chisme
got to, hay que, tener que
gracious, gracia
grave, grave
grease, grasa
greens, verdura
grill, plancha, parilla
grocer's shop, ultramarinos, tienda
'guichet', taquilla, ventanilla
guide, guión

habit, to be in the — of, soler
haddock, merluza
half-way, mitad
halibut, lubina
hallo, adiós, diga, oiga, hola, tal
ham, jamón
hammer, martillo
handbag, bolso
handle, mango, palanca, palo
handy, to come in, venir bien
hang, hang up, colgar, cortar
happen, pasar, resultar
harm, there's no harm done, nada
harp, arpa
have to, to, hay que, tener que
to let —, facilitar
hazel-nut, avellana
heading, encabezamiento
headlight, faro
healthy, sano
hear, I won't — of it!, hablar, va
hearts (cards), copas, corazones
heave, to, echar
heaven, for —'s sake!, anda, hombre
hell!, hablar, vamos
help, facilitar, remedio
there's no — for it, remedio
hemi - demi - semi - quaver, semifusa
hen, gallina
'here!, soy yo
here he comes!, ya
we go!, vámonos
you are!, coger
herring, arenque
high, alto
hinder, dificultar
hire, to, alquilar
hit, to, pegar
hold, to get — of, coger, conseguir
honest, confianza, honesto
honey, miel
'honey', cariño
honour, honor
hope, esperar
horn (car), bocina, claxon

horn, French, trompa
  English, corno inglés
horror, horrible, asqueroso,
  miedo
hors d'œuvres, entremeses
hose-pipe, manga
how, así, como, cosa, estar, tal
how . . .!, cosa
  do you do?, encantado
  do *you* **know?,** saber
  d'you like that?, parecer
  about?, tal
  are you?, tal
  disgraceful!, vergüenza
  much?, vale
  'how-d'you-do', trastorno
hub-cover, tapa
hurt, duele
hyphen, guión

I am . . ., soy yo
  don't **think!,** sí sí
  get it!, caigo
  know, ya
  think, según, digo
I'll say!, hombre
I'll see you, querer
I'm going crazy!, volver
I **see,** ya
ice, helado
ice-box, nevera
ice-cream, helado, mantecado
idea, not a bad, venir bien
ignition, encendido
  key, llave
ignore, to, ignorar, caso
ill-mannered, feo
imagine, just —!, fijarse
important, categoría, importar
incidentally, paréntesis, propósito
including, inclusive
indecent, feo
indeed yes!, hombre
inform, enterar
ingenious, ingenioso
inner-tube, cámara
interfere, dificultar, meterse
interval, descanso
invaluable, apreciable

inventory, inventario
inverted commas, comillas
invoice, albarán, factura
iron, plancha
irritating, fastidiado
-ish (suffix) (see note on
  Diminutive, p. 12)
is . . . there?, estar
isn't it . . .!, cosa
issue, to, repartir

jack (cards), sota
  (cars), gato
jam, mermelada
'jaw', to, charla
job, trabajo, labor
joke, broma, chiste
joker, comodín
jot down, to, apuntar
jug, jarro
junction, empalme
just as if, plan

keep still!, quieto
key, llave, tecla, tonalidad
kettle, cafetera, tetera
kettledrum, timbal
kind, amable, cariño
kindly, cariño
king (cards), rey
kitchen range, fogón
knave (cards), sota
knickers, bragas
knight (cards), caballo
know, not to, ignorar
  I **know,** ya
  you —, sabe
  how should I —?, sabe
  one never —s, sabe

lack of, falta
ladder, escala
  (stocking), carrera
ladies and gentlemen,
  público
lamp, lámpara, bombilla
landlord, dueño

'langoustine', cigala, gamba
lard, manteca
large, largo
larger, mayor
'lark', broma
last, otro
later, luego
lazy, vago
lead (cards), mano
leading-note, sensible
least, at, menos
leave alone, to, soltar
lecture, conferencia
left, to be, quedar
  to be — over, sobrar
lemon, limón
let, to — have, facilitar
  —'s go!, vámonos
  —'s see!, ver
  — go, to, soltar
letter-case, cartera
lettuce, lechuga
lid, tapa
light, lumbre
light, to, encender
lighter, mechero
like, así, como
like, to, convenir, querer
  to be —, parecer
  to feel —, ganas
  to look —, sonar, parecer
  how d'you — that!, parecer
likely, indicado
lime chloride, lejía
list, relación
loaf, pan
lobster, langosta, gamba
lock up, to, echar
lock-up garage, jaula
long, largo
look, parecer
  like, to, parecer, sonar, cara
  out!, ¡cuidado!
  have a — at, echar, ver
  by the — of things, visto
lose one's way, despistar
loud, fuerte
love, to, querer
  I — it!, encantado
lovely, encantado

low, bajo, chiste, grave
luck, with any, mejor
luggage-grid, portaequipajes
lunch, comida

maddening, barbaridad
major, mayor
make, to (cards), barajar
  to, dar
  most of, to, aprovechar
  note of, to, apuntar
man, my good —!, hijo,
  hombre
manage, to — to, conseguir,
  salir, tirar
marmalade, mermelada
marrow (veg.), calabacín
marrow (bone), tuétano
marvellous, estupendo
mashed, puré
mat, estera
match, cerilla
materialise, realizarse
matter, importar
  what's the —?, pasar
  it doesn't —, dar, igual
mayonnaise, mayonesa
meal, comida
mean, medio
  I —, digo, sea
meat, carne, fiambre
meddle, to, meterse
mediant, mediante
medium, medio
meet, encontrar, quedar,
  esperar
mention, don't — it, Dios,
  falta, nada
menu, minuta
mess, lío
message, recado
messenger, botones, recadero,
  ordinario
meter (gas, elec.), contador
'meunière', molinera
middle, medio, mitad
milometer, cuentakilómetros
mind, to, importar
  never —!, dar

mind, I don't, dar, mismo, igual
— **your own business!,** meterse
minim, blanca
minor, menor
mint, menta
'misère', nulos
misfortune, desgracia, pena
misled, despistar
miss, to, echar
molest, lata
moment, rato
  in a —, luego, rato
money, to get the — for, cobrar
more, one, otro
  there isn't any —, quedar
moreover, además, inclusive
mortar, almirez
most, to make — of, aprovechar
motor-bike, moto
mouthpiece, micrófono
movement (music), tiempo
much, not so—, menos
  so — as, sino
  how —?, vale
muck-up, fracaso, lío
mudguard, aleta, guardabarro
mushroom, champiñón, seta
must, falta, hay que, tener que
mustard, mostaza
my dear!, mona

nail, clavo
name and address, señas
nasty, feo
naturally, claro, desde luego
necessary, falta
neck, cuello
necklace, collar
need, falta, hay que, importar
negative, cliché
neither, tampoco
'n'est-ce pas?', verdad
never mind!, dar
news, actual

next, luego, otro
nice, amable, bonito, cariño, simpático
  not nice, feo
nice-looking, guapa, mona
night, last, anoche
nightdress, vestido
no, hablar, parecer, tampoco, st . . . st . . . st . . .
no bid, pasar
  trumps, sin triunfos
nonsense!, va
not a —!, absoluto
  a bit of it!, hablar, va
  at all!, nada, falta
  bad, regular, venir mal
  done, feo, visto
  even, ni siquiera
  so much, menos
note, to make a — of, apuntar
nothing doing, hablar
  much, vamos
  to be done about it, remedio
notice, to take, caso
'nouveau-riche', cursi
now, ya
nuisance, fastidiado, lata, molestar
  to make a — of oneself, dar, lata
number plate, matrícula
nut (engineering), tuerca

obey, to, caso
obstruct, to, dificultar
obtain, to, conseguir
obvious, indicado
obviously, claro
octave, octava
odd, pico, raro, tanto
odds, it makes no, dar, igual, vamos
off we go!, adelante
  season, descanso
  to take —, quitar
office, despacho, oficina
often, menudo
Oh yeah!, sí sí
oil, aceite

oil-seal, retén
O.K., arreglar, vale
older, mayor
olive oil, aceite
omelette, tortilla
on, what's —?, echar
on top, encima
one-way traffic, dirección
onion, cebolla
only too pleased, encantado
opinion, in my, digo, según
opposite, adelante
orange, naranja
ordinary, corriente, regular
orgy, juerga
other side, volver
other day, the, otro
ought, hay que
our, eso, esto
out, to throw, echar
  to pour, etc., echar
outer case (tire), cubierta
outrageous, vergüenza
oven, horno
over there, eso, esto
owner, dueño
oyster, ostra

pack (cards), baraja
pants, calzoncillos
paper-weight, pisapapeles
  -fastener, grapa
paragraph, párrafo
pardon me!, perdone
park, to, estacionar, aparcar
parsley, perejil
parsnip, chirivía
particulars, señas
partridge, perdiz
party, juerga
paste, pastry, pasta
pause, descanso
pause (music), calderón
pay, to get paid, cobrar
  attention, to, caso, atender
peach, melocotón, paraguaya
peanut, cacahuete
pear, pera

peas, guisantes
peculiarities, señas
pedal, pedal
people, gente
perform, realizar, verificar
pestle, mano de almirez
petrol, gasolina
petrol-tank, depósito
pheasant, faisán
pick up, to, coger, recoger
  (tel.), descolgar
picture, in the, confianza
pigeon, pichón
pillow, almohada
pincers, tenazas
'pinch', to, quitar, restar
pipes, cañería, tubería
piston, pistón
  -ring, segmento
pity, pena
plaice, platija
plate, plato
play, jugar, tocar
please, ruego
  do!, Dios, falta
  only too pleased!, encantado
plenty, sobrar
plug (spark),   bujía
  (basin), tapón
  to — in, enchufar
point, punto
  the — is, caso
  there's no — in, cuenta
poke, to poke one's nose into,
  meterse
polished, mona
pomegranate, granada
popular, éxito, visto, vulgar
popularisation, vulgarización
pork, cerdo
posh, cursi
postal order, giro postal
potato, patata
potter about, to, volver
poultry, ave
power station, central
praiseworthy, plausible
prank, broma
prawn, gamba

preferable, mejor
pregnant, embarazada
present, actual
  to be — at, asistir
'present', soy yo
preserves, conservas
presumably, visto
pretentious, cursi
pretty, bonito, guapa, mona
prevent, prevenir
priceless, precioso
probable, indicado
probably, mejor, seguro
produce, to, dar
profit by, to, aprovechar
prospectus, prospecto
provide with, to, proporcionarse
prunes, pasas
public, público
pull one's leg, to, pelo
  out, to, sacar
pullover, pullover
pump, bomba
  to, hinchar, dar aire
  to (metaph.), sacar
punch, taladro
puncture, pinchazo
purpose, on, propósito
push off to, to, quitarse
push out, to, echar
  off the track, to, despistar
put away, to, colocar
  into, to, meter
  on, to, poner, meter
  out, to, poner, meter
  in place, to, colocar
  right, to, arreglar
  through to, to, poner con
  brake on, to, echar

quarrel, pelea
quaver, corchea
quick-tempered, genio
quiet, quieto, suave
  to keep —, callarse
quite so!, claro, desde luego
quite (see note on Diminutive, p. 12)

race-course, carrera
'racket', trampa
radiator, radiador
rag, trapo
  wet —, polvo
rails, off the, despistar
raisins, pasas
raspberry, frambuesa
rather!, hombre (see also note on Diminutive, p. 12)
rations, suministro
reading, lectura
realise, to, cuenta, ignorar, realizar
really, realmente
  can't you —?, como
reason, for that very —, eso
record (gramophone), disco
red, tinto
red currant, grosella
  mullet, lubina, salmonete
re-double, redoblar
reel, bobina
refreshment, refresco
refrigerator, nevera
register, matrícula, registro
regular, regulate, regular
relative, relation, relación
relaxation, descanso
release, soltar
reliable, formal
relief, descanso
remain, to, quedar, sobrar
remedy, remedio
remember, cuenta
remind, sonar
remove, quitar
rent, alquiler, renta
respectable, apreciable
rest, descanso, silencio (music)
restaurant, tasca
result, resultar
reverse, marcha atrás
revolting, asqueroso
ribbon, cinta
rice, arroz
right away, cuanto antes, seguida
  in the middle of, mitad
  that's —!, eso, vale

ring, anillo
  to —, llamar, tocar, sonar
  off, to, colgar, cortar
  up, to, llamar
roast, asado
roll, barra, bollo, suizo
roll-top desk, buró
roller, rodillo
room, to have — for, caber
rope, cuerda
  ladder, escala
round about, alrededor, eso
routine, corriente
row, jaleo, lío, pelea
rubber (bridge), juego
rude, ordinario
rug, manta
ruin, to, polvo
ruler, regla
run (music), glisado, fermata

safe, caja
salad, ensalada
salmon, salmón
salt, sal
same again, mismo, igual
  it's all the —, dar, igual, mismo
  same old, siempre
  the — to you, igual
sand, asperón
sane, sano
sardine, sardina
sauce, salsa, caradura
saucepan, cacerola, cazo, olla
saucer, platillo
sausage, salchicha
savings bank, caja
. . . says, según
say, I should — so!, hombre
  you don't —!, vaya, diga, hombre
scale, escala
scandal, vergüenza
scared, susto
scissors, tijeras
screw, tornillo
screwdriver, destornillador
sea, to be all at, despistar

sea-food, mariscos
sea-sick, mareado
seat, asiento
'second house', tarde
see, _I_ see!, caigo
  let's see, ver
  I'll — you!, querer
seem, parecer
self-starter, arranque, puesta en marcha
sell, to, proporcionar
semibreve, redonda
  -colon, punto y coma
  -quaver, semicorchea
  -tone, semitono
send off, to, expedir
sensible, sensible
sensitive, sensible
sentiments, them's my —!, digo, según
serve, to (tennis, etc.), sacar
set out, to, colocar
settle, to, arreglar, concretar, quedar
sewer, alcantarillas
sh . . .!, quieto
shame, pena, vergüenza
share out, to, repartir
sharp (music), sostenido
shatter, to, polvo
sheet, sábana
shellfish, mariscos
sherry, jerez
shirt, camisa
shock, susto
shock-absorber, amortiguador
shop, tienda
'shop', oiga
shopping, compras
short, in, sea
shorthand, taquigrafía
shove, echar
shovel, recogedor
show, to, enseñar
  me!, ver
shrimp, quisquilla, gamba
shuffle, to, barajar
shut up, to, callarse
sick, mareado
  to be — of, harto

side, cara
  other —, volver
sidelights, faro, luz
silent, to keep, callarse
similar, parecer
simple, simple
simple-minded, simple
since, ya que
single-desks, solistas
  -spacing, espaciador
sink, fregadero
skate, patinar
skid, despiste, patinazo
sleeve, manga
  (cylinder), camisa
slice, rebanada
slightest, not in the, absoluto
slipper, zapatilla
slot, ranura
slow, lento
slum, suburbio
small, chico
  fry, gente
smart, cursi, listo
'smashing', estupendo
Smith, Jones and Robinson,
  Fulano
smoked, ahumado
snacks, aperitivos
snails, caracoles
snobbish, cursi
so, así, resultar, tal
  -so, regular, corriente
  -and-so, fulano, chisme, tal
  much as, sino
  on and so forth, saber,
    tal
  that, resultar, manera
  what?, luego
'sock', to, pegar
socks, calcetines
sofa, sofá
soft, suave
sole, lenguado
something like that, así,
  parecido
some time after, pico
somewhat (see note on
  Diminutive, p. 12)

somewhere about, alrededor,
  eso
son, sonny, hijo
soon, cuanto antes
sore, to be, duele
sorrow, pena
sorry!, perdone
'sort of way', plan
soup, caldo, sopa
space-key, espaciador
spanner, llave
spare, repuesto, sobra, reserva
sparking-plug, bujía
spatula, espumadera
'speaking' (tel.), soy yo,
  hablar
speedometer, cuentakiló-
  metros, indicador
spend, to, tirar
spinach, espinacas
sponge-cake, bizcocho
spool, bobina
spring, ballesta, muelle
  -pin, bulón
squabble, pelea
squids, calamares, chipirones
stake, to, apostar
stand, to, estar
starry-eyed, cariñoso
start, to, empezar
  up, to, arrancar
stave (music), pentagrama
stay, to, quedar
steering, dirección
  -wheel, volante
stencil, cliché
stew, estofado
stick, palo
stick, to, echar, pegar
still, keep —!, quieto
  but —, vamos
stockings, medias
stop, to, parar
story, piso
stove, fogón
strawberry, fresa
strike, to, pegar
strike, to (clock), dar
string, cuerda
stroke, barra

strong-box, caja
subtract, to, restar
suburb, suburbio
succeed in, to, éxito, conseguir
with, to, realizar
success, éxito
such, tal
sucking (pig), cochinillo,
lechal
suddenly, repente
suit (cards), palo
(clothes), traje
to —, convenir
suit-case, maleta
summarise, to, concretar
supper, comida
supply, to, facilitar, suministro
suppose, I — so, visto
surplus, sobrar
surroundings, ambiente
suspenders, ligas, tirantes
sweet, postre
sweetheart, cariño
swipe, to, pegar
switch off, to, apagar, parar
on, encender
swoon, desmayo
sympathetic, simpático

table-cloth, mantel
tail-lamp, piloto
take, to, llevar, tirar
aim, to, apuntar
away, to, quitar, restar
care, to, cuidado
in four, to (music), llevar
a (certain) time, tirar
note of, to, apuntar
notice, to, caso
off, to, quitar
out, to, sacar
place, to, realizar
tangle, lío
tap, grifo
tape, cinta
tart, tarta
tavern, tasca
tea, té

tea-pot, tetera
teacher, profesor
tease, to, meterse
tell us!, chiste
temper, -ament, genio
tempo, tiempo
tenant, inquilino
terribly . . . (see Superlative
p. 13)
terrific, hacha, estupendo
test, to put to the, probar,
verificar
thank goodness!, menos mal
that, eso, esto
's right!, eso
's me, soy yo
's to say, sea
's why, eso
sort of way, plan
how d'you like—!, parecer
then, to be, luego
there, to be, estar
so —!, fastidiado
-abouts, alrededor, así
thick soup, sopa
thing, the done —, visto
the — is, caso
thingummybob, chisme
think, I, digo, según
I — so, parecer
I should — so, hombre
I don't —!, sí sí
what do you —?, parecer
'thirties', the, tantos
this, that, eso esto
throw out, to, echar
away, to, tirar
thumb-tack, chincheta
thus, así
ticket-office, taquilla, ventanilla
tie, corbata
tie-up, lío
'tight', mareado
tile, azulejo
to go on the tiles, juerga
time, it's — to, tener que
'timps' (music), timbal
tin, bote, lata
today, ya

tomato, tomate
tone, tono
tongue, to hold one's, callarse
tonic, tónica
tonight, anoche
top, on, encima
touch, tocar
tough, caradura
traduce, traducir
traffic, one-way, dirección
transfer, trasladar
transformer, bobina
translate, traducir
tray, bandeja
treble, tiple
trick (cards), baza
trill, trino
triplet, tresillo
trombone, trombón
trouble, molestar, pena
  the trouble is, caso
trousers, pantalones
trout, trucha
trumpet, trompeta
trumps, pinta, triunfo
trunk, baúl
trunk call, conferencia
trust, ruego
trustworthy, confianza, formal
try, to, intentar, probar
tuba, tuba
tubes, tubería
tumble, to — to, cuenta, caigo
tunny-fish, atún
turbot, rodaballo
turkey, pavo
'turn', susto
  into, to, convertirse
  out, to, resultar, salir
  over, to, volver
  round, to, dar, volver
  whose — is it?, tocar
turning (street), bocacalle
turnip, nabo
'twenties', the, tantos
twins, gemelos
type, to, escribir
typewriter, máquina
  ribbon, cinta
typist, mecanógrafo

tyre, neumático, cubierta

ugly, feo
unaware, ignorar
underpants, calzoncillos
undershirt, camiseta
understand, entender, coger
undoubtedly, caber
unfortunately, desgraciadamente
universal joint, cruceta
unless, sino
unnecessary, falta
unpleasant, feo
unpopular, visto
unscrupulous, caradura
up-beat, anacrusa
uproar, jaleo
use, to, aprovechar
usual, corriente, siempre

vague, vago
valuable, apreciable
valve, válvula (eng.), pistón
  (music)
vegetables, legumbres, verdura
verify, verificar
vest, camiseta
vile, asqueroso
villa, suburbio
vinegar, vinagre
violent, violento
vulgar, ordinario, vulgar

wait for, to, encontrar, esperar
walk, andar
  up, to, subir
  take a little —, to, volver
wallet, cartera
wangle, trampa
want, to, convenir, ganas,
  querer
  feel — of, to, echar
warn, to, prevenir
wash up, to, fregar
wash-out, fracaso
  -basin, lavabo
washer, arandela
water-closet, water, retrete

way, manera, plan
  to lose one's —, despistar
  no two ways about it, remedio
weaving, to get, liarse, fijarse
wee, chico
well, pues, vaya
  all's well, nada
'wet rag', polvo
what, como
  a . . .!, vaya
  a job!, trabajo
  a . . . thing!, cosa
  a pity!, pena, lástima
  a shame, vergüenza
  cheer!, hola, tal
  do you mean . . .!, como
  do you know about it?, saber
  like, tal
  not, saber, tal
  sort of a . . .?, tal
  at — time, al
  -you-may-call-it, chisme
  so —?, luego
what's . . . about it?, como
  going on?, pasar
  it to be?, quedar
  more, además
  on?, echar
whatever happens, maneras
  it may be, tal
wheel, rueda
when, al
  —'s it to be?, quedar

while, a little, rato
white sauce, bechamela
why not?, como
  that's —, eso
wide, largo
wild strawberry, fresa
win, to, ganar
window, taquilla, ventanilla
windscreen, parabrisas
  -wiper, limpiaparabrisas
wing (car), aleta, guardabarro
wining and dining, juerga
wire, hilo
wit, witty, gracia, ingenioso
with, to do —, importar
'wizard', estupendo
wont, to be, soler
wood-wind, viento
work, to, salir
  it doesn't —, éxito
world, for all the, plan
worth, to be, cuenta, merecer, vale
wrong, the — . . ., convenir

yellow duster, gamuza
yes, soy yo, verdad, ya
  sir?, diga, mande
  sir!, sí señor
  I know, ya
  Oh yeah!, sí sí
you don't say!, vaya
younger, menor
your, eso